Unleashing Britain:

Theatre gets real 1955-64

Unleashing Britain:
Theatre gets real 1955-64

Jim Fowler

with Jonathan Gray

V&A PUBLICATIONS

in association with the Theatre Museum

First published by V&A Publications
in association with the Theatre Museum, 2005

V&A Publications
160 Brompton Road
London SW3 1HW

Distributed in North America by Harry N. Abrams, Inc., New York

The moral right of the author has been asserted.

ISBN 1 85177 473 4

Library of Congress Control Number 2005923378

Designed by Nigel Soper
New photography by Paul Robins of the V&A Photographic Studio

Printed in Italy

V&A Publications
160 Brompton Road
London SW3 1HW
www.vam.ac.uk

Front cover illustration:
Waiting for Godot,
London, 1955.
Photograph by
Houston Rogers
**Back cover and
frontispiece:**
Set for *Look Back in
Anger,* London, 1956.
Photograph by
Houston Rogers

Contents

Preface

This book celebrates the ten years 1955–1964 and the cultural explosion which ushered Britain into the modern age. Illustrated from the extensive collections of the Theatre Museum, it features images of a wide range of performance, many of which have not been published before.

Its publication coincides with the 50th birthday celebrations of The English Stage Company at the Royal Court, the writers' theatre that nurtured much of the new talent that changed the face of British theatre. A new generation of writers, actors and directors mixed in the pubs and coffee bars of the King's Road with artists, designers and musicians who were revolutionising taste and fashion. Mary Quant opened her new shop in the King's Road in 1955, clothing a newly affluent generation of young people in the process of establishing their own youth culture. At the same time in London's East End the dominance of middle-class culture and Arts Council support for it was being dented by Joan Littlewood's socialist Theatre Workshop.

Post-war Britain was energised by the arrival of American rock'n'roll, and blockbusting musicals such as *West Side Story* which combined youth culture with a gritty underclass setting. Imported from continental Europe were the uncompromising modernist dramas of Brecht and Beckett, which shook the tradition of the well-made play to its foundations. John Osborne's *Look Back in Anger* was unleashed upon the stage in 1956, its abrasive anti-hero Jimmy Porter embodying the new phenomenon of the angry young man.

The book describes an era of turbulence and innovation, which brought out the latent reserves in the nation, transcending traditional barriers of class, gender, region and race to forge a new British culture.

Geoffrey Marsh
Director, Theatre Museum
May 2005

1 *The Royal Hunt of the Sun*
Robert Stephens as Atahuallpa and Colin Blakely as Pizarro, Chichester Festival Theatre, 1964
Photograph by Angus McBean

'Various labels have been stuck on us – theatre of the Angry Young Man, Dustbin theatre. Why this objection to anger? It means, true enough, passion but passion in an increasingly conformist society must be good. You can't extinguish anger with a label. For me false values and hypocrisy are more sordid than honest attempts to get to the heart of the matter. However we may be bored by the attack by cliché, we rejoice in it too because it means we are getting through, disturbing, challenging – the true function of all live theatre.'

GEORGE DEVINE, 'WHAT WE'RE UP TO AT THE ROYAL COURT'
FROM THE MERMAID THEATRE REVIEW, 1959

1 After the Blitz

George Devine, Artistic Director of the Royal Court, was a forceful advocate of theatre that questioned illusion and received notions of reality. It was under his aegis that the English Stage Company at the Royal Court staged John Osborne's *Look Back in Anger* in 1956. This ushered in an era of new drama that challenged the escapism of post-war entertainment and tackled the reality of post-war, post-colonial Britain with scant regard for the squeamishness of its audience.

Osborne's play articulated the impatience and anger of a generation, and there was still much to be angry about. Britain emerged from the Second World War as the world's biggest debtor nation. Exports stood at 40% of the pre-war level, and with 500,000 houses destroyed and another 250,000 war-damaged, a huge rebuilding programme was urgently needed. Without American financial support, Britain faced what the economist Maynard Keynes termed 'a financial Dunkirk'.

With the Labour victory in the 1945 general election, Clement Attlee used his huge majority in Parliament to implement the most ambitious social programme the UK had ever seen. The 1944 Education Act had already begun to widen access to secondary and higher education, paving the way for the post-war expansion of the universities. In August 1946 the Council for the Encouragement of Music and the Arts (CEMA) became the Arts Council of Great Britain, which established the groundbreaking principle of public subsidy for the arts. The previous year, only a month after the end of the war, the première of Benjamin Britten's opera *Peter Grimes* represented one of the most important nights in British opera history. It showed that, at last, Britain had an opera composer of international importance, and it radically affected the subsequent development of music theatre in the United Kingdom.

Financing the post-war economic programme required still more sacrifice and austerity. Rationing continued until 1954, and many goods remained scarce, including cigarettes, elastic, pepper, fresh and even dried eggs. Clothes rationing lasted until 1947, when Christian Dior's feminine New Look arrived from Paris. The Festival of Britain, which opened in May 1951, was the spectacular showcase to banish austerity blues. It attracted 8 million visitors and regenerated 27 acres of

2 *Peter Grimes*
Peter Pears as Peter Grimes, and Joan Cross as Ellen Orford in the first Covent Garden production in 1947
Photograph by Angus McBean

London's South Bank with 'The Dome of Discovery' and other exciting modernist structures such as the 'Skylon'. Architect Hugh Casson, a prime mover, observed that it succeeded in making 'people want things to be better, and to believe that they could be'. A survivor from the Festival of Britain is the Royal Festival Hall, the first new public building to be constructed in London since the war.

Paradoxically, West End theatre had flourished during and after the war, providing much-needed escape for troops and civilians alike from the war effort. The government created an organisation for touring theatre, the Entertainment National Service Association (ENSA), irreverently known as 'Every Night Something Awful'. Hugh ('Binkie') Beaumont, managing director of leading producer H.M. Tennent, observed to Terence Rattigan, 'It may sound cynical, but the war has been the making of me. Can't complain about a thing. Look at me and look at the Firm. And to think I owe it all to Hitler.' Richard Huggett commented on Beaumont's career:

> In six years he had presented fifty-nine plays in the West End and of
> those only seven had failed: the others had all had good long runs, many
> of over a year and some record-breaking marathons of over a thousand
> performances each. He'd presented over a hundred plays on tour ...
> No other manager in London had done so well, it was an achievement of
> which anybody could be proud.

In the post-war era H.M. Tennent was in its heyday as the top West End producer. Tennent's philosophy of excellence is exemplified by its lavish presentation of Jean Anouilh's play *Ring Round the Moon* at the Globe Theatre in 1950. Translated from French by Christopher Fry, whose play *The Lady's Not for Burning* had just run for 294 performances, it was the young Peter Brook's first major production in Shaftesbury Avenue. Starring Paul Scofield, Claire Bloom and Margaret Rutherford in a ravishing setting designed by Oliver Messel, it ran for 682 performances and is remembered to this day for its beauty. Anouilh was apparently enchanted: 'I had no idea that my little play could look so marvellous. We in Paris have so much to learn from you in London.'

Fifty years on, Peter Brook recalled post-war theatre as the natural extension of West End life:

> good taste ruled every detail ... when the curtain rose, we were drawn
> out of the everyday world into a world of grace and beauty where

3 *Ring Round the Moon*
Paul Scofield (centre) as Hugh and Claire Bloom as Isabelle, Globe Theatre, London, 1950
Photograph by Houston Rogers

The first London production of Jean Anouilh's *Ring Round the Moon* starred Paul Scofield in the dual role of twin brothers and Claire Bloom as a poor ballet dancer, Isabelle. Other roles were played by Margaret Rutherford and Mona Washbourne. The critics regarded the play as lightweight, resembling a masque or variety entertainment, since the plot was paper-thin and conventionally romantic, and the songs gave the whole production the air of an Ivor Novello production rather than a French comedy.

charming people with not-too-intense feelings played out unreal
situations that never reflected the crude realities of life. This suited me
well … I just followed an instinctive wish to make pictures that moved …
my only wish was to conjure up a parallel and more seductive world.

At Covent Garden, Brook had discovered in ballet an elegance and finesse lacking
in the utilitarian post-war world. British ballet was just establishing itself there
with the Sadler's Wells (soon Royal) Ballet production of *The Sleeping Beauty*
designed by Messel. David Webster, manager of Covent Garden Opera, then took
a gamble. Realising that opera lagged behind theatre in accepting the dominance
of the director, he appointed the twenty-two-year-old Brook 'director of opera
production'. But Brook found staff so hidebound by tradition and resistant to his
innovative designs by Salvador Dalí and Georges Wakhevitch that he was branded
experimental and left two years later in 1949.

Although Covent Garden lost this opportunity to match contemporary
developments in Milan and elsewhere, in 1958 it invited Italian film director Luchino
Visconti to direct and design Verdi's *Don Carlos* with an all-star cast and Carlo
Maria Giulini as conductor. Visconti's 'neo-realist' production, with grand settings
inspired by film, revealed the full depth and beauty of a work that had too often been
dismissed as political and over-long. *Don Carlos* was universally acclaimed,
confirming Covent Garden as a leading international opera house. It remained for

4 *Don Carlos*
Royal Opera House,
Covent Garden, 1958
Photograph by Houston
Rogers

The revival celebrated
the 100th anniversary
of the Royal Opera
House.

5 *A Midsummer Night's Dream*
Royal Opera House, Covent Garden, 1961
Photograph by Houston Rogers

This photograph shows John Piper's setting for the first production of Britten's opera *A Midsummer Night's Dream*. Shakespeare's play became the starting point for Britten's exploration of sleep and the importance of dreams. As one critic wrote, 'All the music of sleep and dreams and the woods bewitched, is quite marvellously successful, from the first heaving, snoring sighs which creep out of the orchestra and seem to hang in the air above the magic glade which John Piper has devised.'

6 *Tosca*
Maria Callas as Tosca and Tito Gobbi as Scarpia, Royal Opera House, Covent Garden, 1964
Photograph by Houston Rogers

The contribution Maria Callas made to the revolution in opera production during the 1950s and early 1960s cannot be over-estimated. Callas worked with visually responsive and textually methodical directors such as Luchino Visconti and Franco Zeffirelli, enabling her to redefine works such as *Norma* and *La Traviata* through her dramatically detailed and musically sensitive performances.

three decades a mainstay of its repertoire. Other notable productions included Britten's opera *A Midsummer Night's Dream* in 1961 and Franco Zeffirelli's thrilling 1964 production of Puccini's *Tosca* with Maria Callas and Tito Gobbi. This created such a sensation that it prompted ITV to broadcast the entire Second Act at short notice on *The Golden Hour* to an audience of over 1.5 million viewers.

Before John Osborne arrived in 1956, getting a new play staged commercially in the West End was virtually impossible; according to Robert Bolt, 'one's name was either Rattigan or it was not'. Tennent rejected *Seagulls over Sorrento*, which Hugh Hastings based on his Navy experience, because, as Richard Huggett explained, 'it was part of Binkie's snobbery that he disliked plays about the working classes and if it was about the armed forces as well that made it worse.'

If a producer expressed interest, the Lord Chamberlain was likely to censor subject matter and language that was too realistic. In 1960 a new sense of morality triumphed in the trial of D.H. Lawrence's *Lady Chatterley's Lover* that liberated the novel, but drama remained subject to the Lord Chamberlain's judgement until the abolition of his censorship powers in 1968. Even plays licensed by him ran the gauntlet of audiences and press comments: coverage of the 1959 cockney 'musical' *Fings Ain't Wot They Used T'Be* (see chapter 8) was headlined 'Is this "real life" – or is it plain dirt?' By contrast, Julie Andrews' performance in the role of Eliza Doolittle in Lerner and Loewe's musical *My Fair Lady* – a charming fantasy based on George Bernard Shaw's serious exploration of class in his play *Pygmalion* – was universally acclaimed; one of the biggest hits in Broadway history, the production was a huge success in Britain in 1958.

Post-war British drama continued along a path that American playwright Arthur Miller described as 'hermetically sealed from life'. The poetic theatre of T.S. Eliot and Christopher Fry took drama away from vernacular language and everyday realism. It was American plays, such as Tennessee Williams' *A Streetcar Named Desire*, Arthur Miller's *Death of a Salesman* (both premièred in the UK in 1949) and Eugene O'Neill's *Long Day's Journey into Night*, together with films starring Marlon Brando and James Dean, that turned the tide, inspiring a new fashion for realism in post-war British theatre.

Miller considered that Osborne's *Look Back in Anger* had a 'very American sense of realism', revealing 'an England of outsiders like myself who ironed their own shirts'. He convinced Laurence Olivier, who had regarded the play as a 'travesty on England', that 'it had real life, a rare achievement'. In persuading Osborne to write something for him (the play that became *The Entertainer*), Olivier began to 'turn away from a trivial, voguish theatre slanted to please the upper

7 Julie Andrews
c.1958
Photograph by Houston Rogers

Making her professional début at the age of twelve, Julie Andrews, with her astonishing four-octave range and crystal clear diction, soon became an audience favourite. She made her Broadway début in the 1954 production of Sandy Wilson's British hit musical *The Boy Friend*. In 1956 she created the role of Eliza Doolittle in Lerner and Loewe's musical *My Fair Lady*. Lerner and Loewe went on to write the part of Guenevere in their 1960 show *Camelot* especially for Andrews. Rodgers and Hammerstein paid her the same honour with their 1957 TV musical version of *Cinderella*.

middle class'. His enlarged vision proved vital for the success of the National Theatre after 1963.

The Royal Court under George Devine championed the new realism. In the first season he produced Arthur Miller's *The Crucible*, a potent interpretation of the anti-Communist 'McCarthy Trials' then taking place in America. Devine also made a point of encouraging new talent, and pioneered work by West Indian dramatists Barry Reckord and Errol John (see chapter 9), early plays by Ann Jellicoe, including *The Sport of My Mad Mother* and *The Knack*, which she also directed, and distinguished scenography by female designers Motley and Jocelyn Herbert. Another remarkable figure was the play agent Margaret ('Peggy') Ramsay, who nurtured many Royal Court writers including Arnold Wesker, Edward Bond, Christopher Hampton, Caryl Churchill, Howard Brenton and David Hare.

The Royal Court remains essentially a writers' theatre, where subsidy supports the right to experiment and the 'right to fail'. In contrast to the commercial theatre, it was not essential to pander to popular taste by providing the escapist illusion and spectacle that made for good box office. The move away from theatrical illusion towards authenticity on the stage was paralleled in the drive by film-makers to achieve greater realism by using real locations in films. Devine's deputy at the Royal Court, Tony Richardson, began his career as a TV director. He and John Osborne

8 *Death of a Salesman*
Kevin McCarthy as Biff and Frank Maxwell as Harry, Phoenix Theatre, London, 1949 Photograph by Angus McBean. H.M. Tennent Collection

Arthur Miller's *Death of a Salesman* was a critical success when it opened on Broadway in February 1949. Based on Miller's own experience of the collapse of his father's business during the Great Depression, the New York production, directed by Elia Kazan, quickly transferred to London's Phoenix Theatre.

9 *Long Day's Journey into Night*
Gwen Ffrançon-Davies as Mary and Alan Bates as Edmund, Globe Theatre, London, 1958 Photograph by Angus McBean. H.M. Tennent Collection

Long Day's Journey Into Night was first produced shortly after O'Neill's death in 1953. The success of the play earned him a posthumous fourth Pulitzer Prize, and was soon presented at the Theatre Royal, Haymarket, by H.M. Tennent.

set up Woodfall Films and filmed *Look Back in Anger* (1959), *The Entertainer* (1960) and *A Taste of Honey* (1961). The latter included scenes shot on location in Salford, which prompted Felix Barker in *The Evening News* to comment 'He has done for Manchester what Visconti or Antonioni have done for Milan.'

The singer Adam Faith, aged sixteen in the mid-1950s, recalled young people's growing impatience with the older generation: 'everyone under the age of about twenty was fed up with the idea that the grown-ups knew more, or were any better, than we were.' Young people aged thirteen to twenty-five had £900 million to spend, which was twice the pre-war figure in real terms, according to Mark Abrams. Youth culture had to invent itself and found expression especially through music and fashion. The designer Mary Quant observed, 'Once only the rich, the Establishment, set the fashion ... now it is the inexpensive little dress seen on the girls in the High Street ... in our shops you will find duchesses jostling with typists to buy the same dresses.' She continued, we wanted to go forward, to do something new … the art schools were a great forcing house of talent, not just clothes, but music … design, food, lifestyle, politics, everything … We all hung out as a group in the King's Road, around the Royal Court and drinking espresso in the Fantasy coffee bar. There was John Osborne, Terence Conran, Elizabeth Frink, [David] Bailey and Donovan … there was a great deal of cross pollination going on.

Focusing on the performing arts between 1955 and 1964, this book draws upon the archives of the Theatre Museum and celebrates the fiftieth anniversary both of the British première of *Waiting for Godot* at the Arts Theatre and of the English Stage Company at the Royal Court. American director and critic Charles Marowitz, who lived in the UK from 1956, described how the nation transformed itself during these years:

10 *The Crucible*
Royal Court Theatre,
London, 1956
Photograph by Houston
Rogers

It is a great compliment to the British character that between 1960 and, say, 1973, to be English was to be thought of as being swinging, loose, innovative, experimental, freaky, uninhibited, idealistic, transcendental, off beat and trendy – words which would have been unthinkable in 1950 and incomprehensible a century earlier.

Terence Rattigan,
1955. Photograph by
Angus McBean

AUNT EDNA (aghast): I knew I was wrong when I applauded The Deep Blue Sea. And what conclusion does Mr Rattigan draw from these squalid anecdotes?

YOUNG PERFECTIONIST: From the first, that love unbridled is a destroyer. From the second, that love bridled is a destroyer. You will enjoy yourself.

AUNT EDNA: But I go to the theatre to be taken out of myself!

YOUNG PERFECTIONIST: Mr Rattigan will take you into an intricately charted world of suspense. By withholding vital information, he will tantalize you; by disclosing vital information, he will astound you.

AUNT EDNA: But what information! Sex and frustration!

KENNETH TYNAN, REVIEW OF *SEPARATE TABLES*
BY TERENCE RATTIGAN (1954)

2 Before the Kitchen Sink

Aunt Edna was the brainchild of Terence Rattigan, England's most popular contemporary dramatist in the early 1950s. Middle-class, unmarried and resident in West Kensington, she typified the middlebrow values of the audience he aimed to please. As homosexuality was still a crime and could not be shown or discussed on the commercial stage, Rattigan needed Aunt Edna as a guide to what his audience would accept. But she became a liability when critics like Kenneth Tynan used her (as in the dialogue opposite) to attack *Separate Tables*, Rattigan's play about the extremes of love and frustration. Tynan loathed what he termed 'Loamshire' plays for and about the well-heeled middle classes, but West End and Broadway audiences disagreed. *Separate Tables* proved so successful that it ran opposite *Waiting for Godot* and *Look Back in Anger* in 1955–56 before transferring to New York.

Rattigan adopted Aunt Edna's persona when reviewing *Waiting for Godot*. In the *New Statesman* s/he found it too 'symbolical', lacking in story and character, and like a 1920s Experimental Drama, 'a movement which led absolutely nowhere'. Of *Look Back in Anger*, he observed to a journalist that Osborne's play was in effect saying 'Look, Ma, I'm not Terence Rattigan'. This unwise comment branded him as an enemy of New Wave drama.

What rival attractions did the Royal Court have to contend with in April 1956? *Theatre World*'s 'Quick Theatre Guide' for April is revealing. H.M. Tennent Ltd was offering two quality productions: Enid Bagnold's play *The Chalk Garden*, directed by John Gielgud with a dream cast including Peggy Ashcroft and Edith Evans, and Graham Greene's *The Power and the Glory* with Paul Scofield, directed by Peter Brook. Other attractions included Richard Burton's Henry V and Othello at the Old Vic; Agatha Christie's thrillers *The Mousetrap* and *Spider's Web*; classic musicals, both British (*The Boy Friend* and *Salad Days*) and American (*Kismet* and *The Pajama Game*); Whitehall farce (*Dry Rot*) and variety/revue, including the Crazy Gang (*Joker's Wild*) and the French revue *La Plume de ma Tante*. For good measure, Peter Daubeny had brought over Jean Vilar's Théâtre National Populaire (the French equivalent to Joan Littlewood's Theatre Workshop) with their lively reinterpretation of such classics as Molière's *Don Juan*.

As it happened, in March 1956, Theatre Workshop made its West End début at the Duke of York's Theatre with *The Good Soldier Schweik,* adapted by Ewan MacColl from the Czech novel of Jaroslav Hašek. Led since 1945 by its inspirational director Joan Littlewood, Theatre Workshop was based at the Theatre Royal, Stratford, in London's East End. Having toured extensively in Britain and Europe, Theatre Workshop remained Britain's most European and innovative company, 'utterly anti-establishment, more profoundly so than the Royal Court because really rooted in working-class experience' (Simon Callow).

Schweik lasted just three weeks in central London because, as Howard Goorney explains, it flouted the naturalistic tradition of British theatre, 'which had always managed to insulate itself from the influence of theatrical movements on the Continent. The stylised acting was not to West End taste, and the décor of black and white cartoons on revolving screens was too avant-garde.' The previous summer Joan Littlewood had staged the UK première of Bertolt Brecht's *Mother Courage and Her Children*, paving the way for the landmark London première of his *Threepenny Opera*, which was still running at the Aldwych in April 1956 (see chapter 3).

There were signs of innovation elsewhere too – in revue, for instance. *Cranks*, a great hit at St Martin's Theatre, was devised

11 *Theatre World*
Cover from the April 1956 issue

12 *Theatre World*
Listing of current London shows from the April 1956 issue

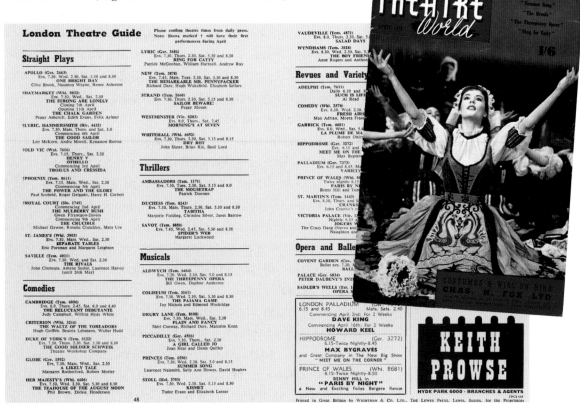

by choreographer John Cranko, with music by John Addison and décor by John Piper. Instead of the large casts, fancy settings and lengthy dialogue customary in revues, *Cranks* featured three young men in jeans and a girl in fishnet tights. They presented a seamless series of songs and dances around the theme of changing identity: 'Am I Marilyn Monroe?/Jean Cocteau?/Marlon Brando/or just dumb crambo?' Premièred at the New Watergate Theatre Club in December 1955 with a cast that included Anthony Newley and black actor Gordon Heath, it transferred to the St Martin's in March 1956, now with Annie Ross. Critic John Barber commented that, 'A revival in English musicals began in a club theatre. A revival in revue could start from this audacious show.' Despite its successful West End run, the show failed to make an impression on Broadway.

If the highlights described are any guide, the West End in April 1956 appeared cool, classy and cosmopolitan, with classic and contemporary British, French, German and American plays and musicals directed by Brook, Hall, Littlewood, Gielgud, Guthrie and others. There are hints of a change in the air but also continuities that survive that change, such as *The Mousetrap*, premièred in 1952 and still running in 2005, or the perennial need to attract American theatregoers to London. Eric Johns was reassured on the latter count in *Theatre World* (June 1956): 'It is good to see so many of our leading actors and actresses playing this year, for apart from Dame Edith and Peggy Ashcroft at the Haymarket, the West End will give visitors a chance to see Sybil Thorndike, Lewis Casson, Paul Scofield, Eric Portman, Margaret Leighton, Vivien Leigh, Alec Guinness, Martita Hunt, Irene Worth, Hugh Griffith, Peggy Mount and lots of others.' If exciting new drama was thin on the ground, acting talent was certainly not.

Theatre in the rest of the UK, though, was in a critical condition. Music hall and weekly rep were dying out, with many repertory theatres reeling from competition with television. The number of theatres with permanent repertory companies shrank from ninety-four in 1950 to fifty-five in 1955, the year that saw the launch of Independent Television. Victorian theatres and music halls were being demolished at the rate of one a week, some claimed. Between 1945 and 1975 at least 324 theatre buildings were lost: 8 in central London, 50 in Greater London and about 266 elsewhere in Britain.

In the mid-1950s, the survival of regional theatre depended on the Arts Council, who devised a ten-year rescue plan described by *Theatre World* (April 1956) as follows: 'if Britain, in ten years time, possessed thirty consolidated theatres, outside London, some of them new buildings and some renovated old ones, the prospects of the living drama might in our time be transformed.'

13 *The Mousetrap*
*Ambassadors Theatre,
London, 1954
Photograph by Houston
Rogers*

After the war the West
End was dominated by
the commercial sector.
Farces and whodunnits
became very popular.
The most famous was

Agatha Christie's *The
Mousetrap*, which
became the longest
running show in West
End history.

14 *Cranks*
*Set design by John
Piper, New Watergate
Theatre, London, 1955*
S.53-2003

The originality and
inventiveness of this
revue, with sets
designed by John Piper,
was not lost on the
critics. John Barber
described how the cast
'played with shoes and
hats, and made patterns
with their hands. And
they caught the mood
of frolic in spring —
or of a wicked love
affair. All of it was new-
minted and at least half
of it was brilliant.'

Timothy Bateson as
Lucky in *Waiting for
Godot*, 1955
Photograph by
Houston Rogers

'Audiences had never before seen anything like the spectacle provided by Waiting for Godot. Its drab, bare scene was dominated by a withered tree and a garbage can.'

HAROLD HOBSON, *THE THEATRE IN BRITAIN*

(1984)

'None of us had any idea of how to begin to tackle [Brecht]. It seemed to me as daunting as doing a Japanese Noh play in weekly rep.'

JOHN OSBORNE, *ALMOST A GENTLEMAN: AN
AUTOBIOGRAPHY, VOLUME II: 1955-1966* (1991)

3 The Avant-garde

Waiting for Godot has become perhaps the most famous post-war play, for no other has so influenced writers and maddened or delighted its audiences. Now a classic, it has not lost its modernist cutting edge.

Samuel Beckett, a forty-two-year-old Irish Protestant, wrote it in French titled *En Attendant Godot* in 1948–49. Beckett had earlier worked as an assistant to James Joyce and had made his name as a novelist in Paris between the wars. Later decorated for bravery in the French Resistance, Beckett fled from the Gestapo into south-east France with his companion Suzanne in 1942. Travelling on forged papers, the couple walked the last 150 miles at night, hiding by day in haystacks. This rootless existence underlay the world of Beckett's characters Vladimir and Estragon. Revisiting his native land after the war, Beckett was dismayed at the feast his family provided in his honour, remarking that 'my friends eat sawdust and turnips while all Ireland safely gorges.'

Beckett had virtually no professional theatre experience when he wrote *En Attendant Godot*. The play lacks a recognisable plot, and its language was shockingly colloquial to French ears. Paris was a hotbed of avant-garde theatre, yet no one would take on his play until Roger Blin premièred it in January 1953. The set, with oil drums and wire-and-paper tree, reflected the tiny budget but accorded with Beckett's desire to pare down to essentials. Simplicity of means in fact masked a complexity that remained as elusive as the identity of Godot and the other characters.

Beckett was wary of attempts to 'explain' his play. He agreed with Blin that Pozzo should be dressed as an English landowner, yet he rejected the idea of staging in the round to reflect the circularity of the action, arguing that this should be implicit rather than physically stated. The play generated fierce controversy that made Beckett famous overnight. To some it was a daring hoax that had to be seen, to others a true 'play of our time' that reflected a bleak post-war world of Cold War and social upheaval.

Eight German cities clamoured to produce the play, and Blin prepared to tour it around France. Beckett, meanwhile, translated it into English as *Waiting for*

Godot for the West End première that Peter Glenville and Donald Albery had planned in 1954. This was seriously delayed, however, when the Lord Chamberlain insisted on censoring the erection-by-hanging and trouser-dropping episodes, and toning down the language. Furthermore, leading actors including Gielgud, Richardson and Guinness could not be persuaded to appear in the play.

Albery offered it instead to Peter Hall to première at the Arts Theatre Club in summer 1955. Although in theory productions at London theatre clubs did not require a Lord Chamberlain's licence, Beckett conceded some changes to ensure that the production went ahead, but he did so under protest and boycotted the first night. An aficionado of French drama, Hall regarded Paris as the centre of theatre and his acceptance of *Waiting for Godot* reflected a policy of showcasing foreign drama so that 'potential British dramatists can see what is happening abroad'. He had already directed *The Lesson,* the first play by Ionesco to be seen in London, Lorca's *Blood Wedding* and O'Neill's epic *Mourning Becomes Electra.*

The first night of *Waiting for Godot,* 3 August 1955, was almost its last, due to an onslaught by the press. Ivor Brown in 'Waiting for Codot' lampooned 'play-going in Puzzle Corner'. Campbell Williams, the proprietor of the Arts Theatre Club, wanted to bury the show there and then, but Hall prevailed on him to wait for the Sunday critics, especially Harold Hobson, whom Hall in the meantime persuaded of Beckett's genius. In the event, Hobson saved the day, along with Kenneth Tynan, who stressed that it was 'a conversational necessity' to have seen the play. Now the talk of the town, the production transferred to the West End and ran profitably at the Criterion theatre until March 1956.

In August 1956 the Berliner Ensemble, founded by Bertolt Brecht on his return from exile to East Berlin in 1949, made its first visit to the UK. Before and during the Second World War, when Brecht's Marxist affiliation made it unsafe to remain in Hitler's Germany, he had pursued his career as a leading director-playwright in Europe and America. He died shortly before the Berliner Ensemble gave their first London season at the Palace Theatre.

Before 1955, Britain's awareness of Brecht was limited to a few pre-war productions and writings. Joan Littlewood's pioneering Theatre Workshop production of *Mother Courage and Her Children* at the Devon Festival, Barnstaple, was followed in February 1956 by the London première of *The Threepenny Opera,* twenty-eight years after Brecht wrote it. *The Threepenny Opera* is based on the English playwright John Gay's *The Beggar's Opera* (1728), with its world of beggars, thieves and prostitutes. Brecht set his version in the modern era, using none of the original music or text except some character names. His targets were the failing politicians of the Weimar Republic as well as capitalist greed. With Kurt Weill's music, including the classic song 'Mack the Knife', Brecht's low-life satire was his first and greatest commercial success.

The Threepenny Opera was running in Mark Blitzstein's version in New York when Oscar Lewenstein, a far left-wing producer involved in forming the English Stage Company, bought the rights to present it in London with Wolf Mankowitz and Helen Arnold. Lewenstein and director Sam Wanamaker visited Brecht and agreed that Caspar Neher, designer of the 1928 production, should design the 1956 UK première, but differently. Neher devised an Edwardian bandstand set for the onstage musicians, while the Street Singer used a blackboard to tell the story. With a budget of £10,000 they hired a strong cast, which included Bill Owen as Mack, Ewan Macoll (Street Singer), Warren Mitchell, and singers Georgia Brown (Lucy) and Mary Remusat (Jenny). After a week's try-out in Brighton, the production ran for almost six months in London at the Royal Court, Aldwych and Comedy theatres, recouping two-thirds of its costs.

Although the Lord Chamberlain censored some risqué language, the realism of the brothel scenes retained its power to shock. The BBC refused to broadcast 'Mack the Knife' for fear of seeming to glamorise violence. The song's title, however, soon provided the popular press with a nickname for the future Prime Minister Harold Macmillan. Billed as 'A Soho Musical', the production's dedication to decadence was welcomed by critic Milton Shulman as an antidote to *Salad Days*. But he suspected that some of Brecht's caustic satire had been lost in the process: 'It hardly seems possible that this high-spirited romp was ever considered a left-wing social protest. Its abandon and anarchy is now surely deviationist.'

Brecht was a Marxist moralist who condemned bourgeois conventions, and held that theatre should reflect and criticise life. His influence on European directors and playwrights, including his advocacy of ensemble values, was at its height in the 1960s and 1970s.

17 *Waiting for Godot*
*Peter Woodthorpe as
Estragon (left), Peter
Bull as Pozzo and Paul
Daneman as Vladimir,
Arts Theatre Club,
London, 1955
Photograph by
Houston Rogers*

Director Peter Hall
confessed that he had
no idea what some of
the text meant, 'but if we
stop and discuss every
line we'll never open. I
think it may be
dramatically effective
but there's no hope of
finding out till the first
night.' Actor Peter Bull
admitted that he was
less afraid when
landing on the Italian
beach-heads during the
Second World War than
facing the opening
night audience. The
audience's hostility was
only too clear, and a
mass exodus began
soon after the play's
start. The daily
newspapers damned
the play, but once
Kenneth Tynan in *The
Observer* had told his
readers that *Godot*
would be 'a conver-
sational necessity for
many years' audiences
improved.

18 *Waiting for Godot*
Set design by Peter
Snow, Arts Theatre
Club, London, 1955
S.1132-1984

19–22 *Waiting*
for Godot
Costume designs
by Peter Snow for
Vladimir, Estragon,
Lucky and Pozzo,
Arts Theatre Club,
London, 1955
S.1133–6-1984

Bertolt Brecht and Kurt Weill's *The Threepenny Opera* is a masterpiece of musical theatre that grew out of its writers' bitter experience of Weimar Germany. The song 'Mack the Knife', which has been covered by, among many others, Frank Sinatra and Ella Fitzgerald, was a last-minute addition, written during the rehearsal period.

26 *The Threepenny Opera*
Daphne Anderson as Polly, Bill Owen as 'Mack the Knife' and Georgia Brown as Lucy, Royal Court Theatre, London, 1956
Photograph by Kevin MacDonnell

27 *The Threepenny Opera*
Page from Theatre World, *April 1956*
Photograph by Kevin MacDonnell

"The Threepenny Opera"

at the Aldwych

FIRST presented at the Royal Court on 9th February, Bertolt Brecht and Kurt Weill's "The Threepenny Opera" scored a big hit and has now been transferred to the Aldwych Theatre. Brecht's play, with music by Kurt Weill, is here given in an English adaptation by Marc Blitzstein. Sam Wanamaker produces, the musical direction being under Berthold Goldschmidt and décor by Caspar Neher.

The Prologue which opens the opera, shewing Ewan MacColl as the Street Singer, centre, who is singing the "Ballad of Mack the Knife." In the background is the permanent bandstand which graces the scene, which is set in Soho on the threshold of the twentieth century. To the right is the blackboard with which the Street Singer helps to tell the story.

9

Mem. The particular attention of the Management is called to the following Regulations, which refer to all Stage Plays licensed by the Lord Chamberlain. The strict observance of these Regulations is to be considered as the condition upon which the Licence is signed.

Any change of title must be submitted for the Lord Chamberlain's approval.

No profanity or impropriety of language to be permitted on the Stage.

No indecency of dress, dance, or gesture to be permitted on the Stage.

No objectionable personalities to be permitted on the Stage, nor anything calculated to produce riot or breach of the peace.

No offensive representations of living persons to be permitted on the Stage.

Stage Play Licence
Dated 3 December 195?
Entitled
"The Threepenny Opera"

Theatre
Theatre Royal,
Brighton.

PLEASE SEE ENDORSEMENT

This Licence is issued on the understanding that the following alterations are made:—

1. Act I, page 2, for "up her thigh" substitute "on her thigh".
2.   for "Wonder what got into her" substitute "Wonder what's come over her".
3.   " 9, for "Jesus come and be our host" substitute "Lord save us".
4.   " 10. for "They make love, they make love till the man is through" substitute "They want love, they want love. Then when they have had it she is sorry that she gave in".
5. Scene 2, p.15, for "I only need a certain part of her" substitute "Till she wears out I'm hanging on to her.
6.   p.16. for "keep it up high" substitute "Keep the flag flying old son
7.   p.17, for "Never let a thing go down that ought to stand up" substitute "Never let it drop to half-mast".
8. Act II, scene 2, for "I covered her" substitute "I cared for her".
          p.16.

28 *The Threepenny Opera*
Licence from the Lord Chamberlain's Office for the performances at the Royal Court Theatre, London, 1956 Oscar Lewenstein Collection

The Lord Chamberlain's licence for *The Threepenny Opera* lists several changes to the script that were demanded before the show could be performed on the public stage.

'On May 8, 1956 a theatrical atom bomb was dropped by The English Stage Company on the stage of the Royal Court Theatre ... the hitherto unsuccessful John Osborne saw success come to him overnight, the generation which has adopted aggression as its passport to life found a ready-made excuse for its behaviour, and hundreds of men found themselves dubbed the angry young men. Angry at what? Angry because their grandfathers and fathers had launched the world into two great wars? Angry because of their own incompetence? Or, perhaps, angry at the futility of a life with no apparent hope?'

STREATHAM NEWS (5 APRIL 1957)

4 Angry Young Men

Although the form of *Look Back in Anger* was not as experimental as that of *Waiting for Godot*, its naturalistic technique expressed an intensity of feeling which connected British theatre more directly with everyday life. It represents the British avant-garde in the sense that 'it started a national revolution: the young for the first time wanted to write plays, not novels or poems' (Peter Hall).

An early Royal Court flyer describes *Look Back in Anger* as an 'intensely personal play' and 'a disturbing comment on Osborne's own generation'. Its central character is an English 'Rebel Without a Cause' (a reference to James Dean). The phrase was soon replaced by 'Angry Young Man', an invention of the Royal Court's press officer that instantly conjured John Osborne, his play – whose author, director and lead actors were all in their twenties – and Jimmy Porter's testosterone-laden outbursts. Its shock waves radiated far and wide, rallying a new generation, showing the potency of theatre to speak out in a world of increasing uncertainty.

Osborne disliked the Angry Young Man label, yet could not resist a new car with the number-plate AYM1. Rather than be considered a social critic or spokesman for his generation, he regarded *Look Back* as expressing his concern for personal relations, which 'may have social and moral implications'. He wrote the play in response to a deep personal crisis. After seven years acting and stage-managing in provincial theatre, he was out of work and traumatised by marital breakdown. His autobiography confirms that the play was the product of 'shocked, brooding months' of separation after his first wife Pamela left him for a dentist and the experiences that led to this situation. For instance, he quotes at length Jimmy Porter's account of marrying Alison as a 'fairly accurate description' of his own wedding to his first wife.

Looking back on his mental state in the summer of 1955, Osborne recalled the 'inertia' of post-war Britain as the Empire slipped away and the 'Establishment' clung on. He used *Look Back in Anger* to sum up the tension between the young and older generations as they faced a radically changing nation: 'Jimmy Porter was hurt because things had remained the same. Colonel Redfern grieved that everything had changed. They were both wrong, but that was hard to see at the time.'

Although *Look Back in Anger* was rejected by leading play agents, Osborne believed that something would turn up and was spectacularly rewarded when George Devine agreed to première his play on 8 May 1956 in the first English Stage Company season at the Royal Court Theatre.

Osborne found in Kenneth Haigh a talented actor who could live up to an anti-hero as compelling as Jimmy Porter, and in Tony Richardson a director who gave the 'extremity' of his writing consistency and credibility. During the summer of 1956 *Look Back in Anger* continued to attract critical interest, but by mid-September declining ticket sales almost caused it to close three weeks early. Its fortunes were dramatically revived by a couple of television broadcasts, and it transferred to the West End, and then to New York in 1957.

During autumn of the same year the play toured the theatreless regions of Wales and the north-east in an Arts Council production directed by Frank Dunlop. A reviewer of Colin Jeavons's 'superbly squalid' performance as Jimmy Porter noted 'one of those rare moments in the theatre where an audience is so completely identified with a character that there is, especially in the second act, an overwhelming urge to go and punch the actor on the nose'.

The urge to punch Jimmy anticipated an incident in New York. With *Look Back* ticket sales falling, Osborne remembered how producer David Merrick 'hired an out-of-work actor to get up on the stage and strike Kenneth Haigh in a fit of fury. The audience was delighted, a photographer recorded the event for *Time* magazine, and bookings rose … For $50 it was a stylish investment.' Tony Richardson recalls that the assailant was 'a feminist before her time' and the stunt 'established the play for a year on Broadway and afterwards a year's tour'.

With the success of *Look Back in Anger*, Osborne's name was made, and he went on to write *The Entertainer*, premièred in 1957, which was born of his nostalgia for the music hall. He wrote in his Note to the first edition: 'The music hall is dying, and, with it, a significant part of England. Some of the heart of England has gone; something that once belonged to everyone, for this was truly a folk art.'

Osborne's passion for music hall can be gauged from his habit in later life of listening to artists from the halls on his Walkman and his appreciation of leading comic Max Miller. Although 'Cheeky Chappie' Miller was the apotheosis of music hall on its very last legs, Osborne denied that he was the model for Archie Rice in *The Entertainer*: 'Max didn't have to be lovable like Chaplin or pathetic like a clown. His humanity was in his cheek. Max got fined £5 and the rest of the world laughed with him. Archie would have got six months and no option. I loved Max

because he embodied a kind of theatre I admire most. His method was danger …
danger that he might go too far.'

Osborne found the contact with music hall 'immediate, vital and direct' and its
conventions liberating where they cut across the limitations of the naturalistic
stage. *The Entertainer* alternates dialogue with songs as music hall 'turns'. Music
hall emerges as a symbol for a nation unable to sustain its once great past. Although
Osborne's Note sounds a nostalgic farewell, the play insistently reminds us that
the year is 1957; Jean attends Trafalgar Square rallies about troubles in the Middle
East that claim the life of Archie's son Mick.

Osborne recalled how contemporary events loomed large during completion
of the play in early 1957:

> The muddle of feeling about Suez and Hungary, implicit in *The
> Entertainer*, was so overheated that the involvement of Olivier in the
> play seemed as dangerous as exposing the Royal Family to politics.
> There was some relief that an international event could arouse such
> fierce, indeed theatrical responses, with lifetime readers cancelling the
> *Observer* and rallies and abuse everywhere. The Korean War had come
> and gone like a number two touring company: this one would run on well
> into foreseeable history. The season was open for hunting down
> deceivers and self-deceivers.

Osborne's later plays include *Luther* (1961), in which he turned to history for an
exploration of protest and revolt. The play starred the twenty-four-year-old Albert
Finney as the fiery Martin Luther. As Christopher Innes observes, 'Luther is the
only Osborne anti-hero who qualifies, however ambiguously, as successful in
smashing a complacent society.'

Royal Court Theatre

Sloane Square S.W.1

Licensed by the London County Council to Alfred Esdaile

English Stage Company

Artistic Director George Devine

Clare Austin   Willoughby Gray   Alec McCowen
Gary Raymond   Anna Steele

October 28th to November 23rd

Four Weeks Only

LOOK BACK IN ANGER

by

John Osborne

Original Production by Tony Richardson
Directed by John Dexter

Setting: Alan Tagg   Music: Thomas Eastwood

All Seats bookable 5/-, 7/6, 10/6 and 15/-
Box Office SLOane 1745
Mon. to Fri. 7-30   Sat. 5 & 8-15   Mat. Wed. 2-30

29 *Look Back in Anger*
Poster for the Royal
Court Theatre, London,
1957
S.24-1983

The English Stage
Company developed a
house style for its
graphics. They used this
format for the poster of
Look Back in Anger and
for all their publicity in
1957 and 1958.

30 *Look Back in Anger*
Kenneth Haigh as
Jimmy, Alan Bates as
Cliff and Mary Ure as
Alison, Royal Court
Theatre, London, 1956
Photograph by Houston
Rogers

Probably no other play
of the last fifty years
has occasioned so
much reaction as *Look
Back in Anger*. It helped
to establish the fame of
the English Stage
Company in its earliest
days.

31 *Look Back in Anger*
*Kenneth Haigh as
Jimmy and Vivienne
Drummond as Helena,
Royal Court Theatre,
London, 1956
Photograph by Houston
Rogers*

32 *Look Back in Anger*
*John Welsh as Colonel
Redfern and Mary Ure
as Alison, Royal Court
Theatre, London, 1956
Photograph by Houston
Rogers*

33 *Look Back in Anger*
*Page from the TV Times
for Wednesday, 28
November 1956,
announcing the ITV
broadcast of the play in
a 90-minute version.*

34 *Look Back in Anger*
*Cast list for a
production performed
in Russia, 1957*

The notoriety of *Look
Back in Anger* meant
that it was very swiftly
performed by European
theatre companies,
even behind the Iron
Curtain.

Слободан Перовић

Ксенија Јовановић

Снимци: Антон Бан

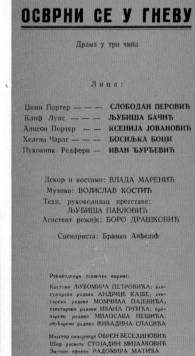

ЏОН ОСБОРН
ОСВРНИ СЕ У ГНЕВУ

Драма у три чина

Лица:

Џими Портер — — — СЛОБОДАН ПЕРОВИЋ
Клиф Лупс — — — ЉУБИША БАЧИЋ
Алисон Портер — — — КСЕНИЈА ЈОВАНОВИЋ
Хелена Чарлс — — — БОСИЉКА БОЦИ
Пуковник Редферн — — — ИВАН ЂУРЂЕВИЋ

Декор и костими: ВЛАДА МАРЕНИЋ
Музика: ВОЈИСЛАВ КОСТИЋ
Техн. руководилац претставе:
ЉУБИША ПАВЛОВИЋ
Асистент режије: БОРО ДРАШКОВИЋ

Сценариста: Бранко Анђелић

Руководиоци техничке опреме:

Костими ЉУБОМИРА ПЕТРОВИЋА; валсуварски радови АНДРИЈЕ КАЈБЕ; столарски радови МОМЧИЛА ПАЈЕВИЋА; тапетарски радови ИВАНА ГРГИЋА; браварски радови МИЛОСАВА ПЕШИЋА; обућарски радови ЖИВАДИНА СПАСИЋА.

Мајстор позорнице ОБРЕН ВЕСЕЛИНОВИЋ
Шеф расвете СТОЈАДИН МИЈАЛКОВИЋ
Звучни ефекти РАДОМИРА МАТИЋА

Љубиша Бачић

Босиљка Боци

Иван Ђурђевић

SPOTLIGHT on next week's play—and it reveals—

An excuse for a generation

ON May 8, 1956, a
theatrical a to m
bomb was dropped by
The English Stage Com-
pany on the stage of
The Royal Court
Theatre in London's
picturesque Sloane
Square.

Actors, audience and
theatre withstood the shock
but as reverberations were
felt so far afield that reputed
moved in from all over the
civilised world for months
seem to produce John
Osborne's remarkable play
"Look Back in Anger."

The sudden sensational John
Osborne was instant cause to the
newcomer, the prim...

Jocelyn Britton as "Alian Porter" the wife of the angry young man, and Michael Bryant as "Cliff Lewis" that joined in a scene from the play.

Walked Seven Miles After Marlowe Show

One of the finest compliments
paid to the high standard of
Marlowe Repertory productions
was contained in a letter received
by the manager, Mr Alan Gray.
It was from Mrs. I. M. Clarke, of
Tankerton, who wrote to say how
very much she and her husband
had enjoyed a performance of
Look Back in Anger at an en-
joyment which by no way had
been lessened by the fact that
having missed their last bus, they
had walked the seven miles back
to Tankerton, arriving home at
1.30 a.m.

Angry Young Man at Bromley

**Bromley Repertory production of " Look Back In Anger ", with
Cherry Morris. Sheila Hancock and Tony Beckley**

TEN YEARS' SUCCESS STORY

Scunthorpe actress stars with Olivier

A MODEST, 27-YEAR-OLD, Scunthorpe-born woman, who is
rapidly making a name for herself on the West End stage,
has achieved the aim of hundreds of actresses—she will
play opposite Sir Laurence Olivier.

She is Joan Plowright, who has just begun rehearsals at
London's Royal Court Theatre for "The Entertainer," in which
Sir Laurence has the lead.

Her career has been a steady
but sure rise to stardom. Some
10 years ago, when she left
Scunthorpe Grammar School
her only stage experience was
in end-of-term productions and
amateur group work.

Even in her earlier days at
Henderson-ave Junior School
Miss Plowright had been "keen
on acting," and her father, Mr
W. E. Plowright, of 6, West
Common-gdns, a Scunthorpe
journalist, always encouraged
her ambition.

JOAN PLOWRIGHT

AT MANCHESTER

She went to a Manchester
drama school for a year and in
1948 joined the training school
attached to the Old Vic theatre.

In 1950, she went into reper-
tory for a year and joined the
Old Vic Company for a South
African tour in 1951.

During this visit, Miss Plowright became engaged to
another member of the company, Mr Roger Gage, and
they were married at Scunthorpe in 1953.

TELEVISION LEAD

She had a number of tele-
vision engagements in 1954,
including the singing lead in a
musical version of Sheridan's
"The Duenna," and the part of
Adrianna in Shakespeare's
"Comedy of Errors".

Miss Plowright was also with
the Bristol Old Vic Company
and had a successful season in
repertory at Nottingham with
her husband.

Her big stage chance came in
1955 when she was chosen to
play the mad cabin boy in
"Moby Dick," with Orson
Welles.

CRITICS' PRAISE

At the end of 1956 she was
praised by London critics for
her performance in the title role
of "The Country Wife." She
co-starred in this production
with Laurence Harvey.

Her success in "The Chairs"
this year involved a complete
switch of character from the
girl wife in "The Country
Wife" to a 90-year-old woman.

Miss Plowright's film career
to date amounts to a 5sec.
appearance in "Gilbert and
Sullivan" some years ago.

REFUSED FILM OFFER

She turned down the offer of
a film contract with the Rank

and she has recently refused an
offer to work in America.

Miss Plowright's view is that
she is not sufficiently established on the London stage to
risk a year's absence across the
Atlantic.

SCUNTHORPE IS "HOME"

Although her busy theatrical
life does not nowadays allow
her much time to visit Scunthorpe, she still refers to the
town as "my home."

A Scunthorpe friend of Miss
Plow...
in an...
pays...
is sti...
Succe...
to her...
I don'...

---

35 *Look Back in Anger* and *The Entertainer*
Selection of newspaper cuttings for regional theatre productions
English Stage Company Archive

During 1957 *Look Back in Anger* was performed in many theatres around Britain, not only in the touring version of the Royal Court production (with Michael Bryant and Alan Dobie) but in new productions at the Bristol Old Vic (with Richard Harris), Bromley Repertory Theatre (with Sheila Hancock) and the Marlowe Theatre, Canterbury.

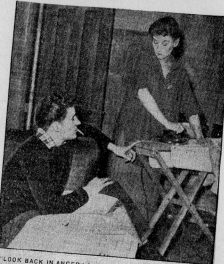

"LOOK BACK IN ANGER," John Osborne's controversial play about
young people, has its first repertory performance at Bristol's
Theatre Royal today. In this scene, taken at yesterday's dress
rehearsal, are Peter O'Toole, as Jimmy Porter, and Phyllida Law, as
Helena Charles.

AN ANGRY YOUNG MAN COMES TO THE FOOTLIGHTS

*ALAN DOBIE (left) plays the part of
Jimmy Porter, the hero of John Osborne's
remarkable play "Look Back in Anger."
Yorkshire-born Alan celebrates his 25th
birthday to-morrow.*

A NGRY YOUNG MEN—the intellectual equivalent of the Crazy
Mixed-Up Kids—owe their fame to John Osborne, author of Look
Back in Anger, which opens at the Opera House next week.
Was the label first attached to Osborne himself or to Jimmy Porter, the leading
character in his play?

We don't mind predicting that quite a
few Ambitious Young Playwrights will
try to repeat the success of 27-year-old
Osborne by creating more Angry Young
Men in the near future.

The part of Jimmy Porter, the young
man of shattered illusions who cannot help
himself from deliberately hurting those he
loves, is played by Alan Dobie.

Alan joined the London Old Vic School in
1952 with the intention of becoming a
scenic designer, but before he had reached
that part of his course the school had closed.
So he remained an actor.

He has appeared in numerous Old Vic
productions both in Bristol and London.

Green-eyed Jocelyn Britton, who plays
opposite him in "Look Back in Anger"
began her career as a ballet dancer and has
danced with the Ballet Rambert and the
Festival Ballet.

Though only 22, she has played in several
London productions, has spent one season
with the Shakespeare Memorial Theatre,

Stratford-on-Avon, and enjoyed the thrill of
a trip to America with the Old Vic in "A
Midsummer Night's Dream."

Hubert Wilmot and the Arts Theatre
company appreciated the impulse which
prompted a member of the audience to send
a note during the interval at a recent performance of "A View from the Bridge." It
read: "To the cast and producer: Con-
gratulations on a fine job. I look forward to
the second part."
It was signed Karl Ford, New Haven,
Connecticut.

Mr. Ford, who is a member of the drama
department of Yale University, was visiting
Dublin for the theatre festival and came to
Belfast to see Arthur Miller's play.

Another ballet dancer who is out to make
a name for herself is 18-year-old Margaret
Craig of Glasgow.

She is one of the eight-strong Emplrelles
dancing troupe featured in the new edition
of the revue **Brightly Nighty** at the Empire.
This will run for a five-week
season from Monday.
Margaret will be taking a leading role in
several sequences, among which is one called
"The Fountains of Rome."
Heading the bill is knock-about comedian
Danny Cummins.

*JOAN COLLINS, who plays the title role in
"Sea Wife" is one of four survivors from a
shipwreck. Only one of the three other
occupants of a raft knows that she is a nun.
"Sea Wife" is set on the sea and on a
desert island.*

---

36 *Look Back in Anger*
Kenneth Haigh as Jimmy, Royal Court Theatre, London, 1956
Photograph by Houston Rogers

The character of Jimmy Porter, as portrayed by Kenneth Haigh, was seized upon by many in the media as the symbol of a generation of disaffected, university-educated young men at odds with 1950s Britain.

37 *The Entertainer*
Set design by Alan
Tagg, Royal Court
Theatre, London, 1957
British Council
Collection
S.2442-1986

Alan Tagg accepted an
invitation to design for
the English Stage
Company from George
Devine and Tony
Richardson in 1956.
His first play at the
Royal Court Theatre
was John Osborne's
Look Back in Anger.

38 *The Entertainer*
Costume design by
Clare Jeffery for
Laurence Olivier as
Archie Rice, Royal
Court Theatre,
London, 1957
S.415-1987

39 *The Entertainer*
Laurence Olivier
as Archie Rice.
Photograph by
Snowdon

40 *The Entertainer*
Double page from an
article in Picture Post,
20 April 1957,
featuring the première
at the Royal Court
Theatre. Photographs
by Roger Wood

OSBORNE: 'I couldn't have had a better cast for my play.'
OLIVIER: 'I am proud to appear in it.'

Photographed by ROGER WOOD

A NEW SIR LAURENCE: BLUE JOKES AND PATRIOTIC SONGS ARE THE MAIN PROPS OF ARCHIE RICE'S GRUESOME COMEDY ROUTINE IN HIS 'ROCK 'N' ROLL NEW'D LOOK' REVUE.

Osborne's Gift to Olivier

'The Entertainer' proves John Osborne to be Britain's
only great young dramatist, and allows Sir Laurence
Olivier to give one of his most profound performances as a broken-down music-hall comedian.

Picture Post, April 20, 1957

OVER

Lynn Seymour and
Desmond Doyle, 1960
Photograph by
Houston Rogers

'For years we have
longed for a new wave
in British ballet,
comparable to that
which has reanimated
the spoken drama. Well,
MacMillan has done
something new: he has
dealt directly with a
real and tragic event.'

RICHARD BUCKLE, REVIEW OF *THE INVITATION*

(JANUARY 1961)

5 Steps in the Right Direction

Kenneth MacMillan was born in Dunfermline and raised in Great Yarmouth. He danced with the Sadler's Wells Theatre Ballet and the Sadler's Wells Ballet at Covent Garden from 1946 to 1955 – the year in which *Danses Concertantes* established him as a major choreographer. Though influenced by the French dance of Roland Petit, early works such as *Laiderette* (1954) and *Noctambules* (1956), about a hypnotist scorned by an audience, reflect MacMillan's life-long concern with 'outsiders'. As he said, 'The more I look at my work the more it seems that, unwittingly, I choose the lonely, outcast, rejected figure.'

A lover of theatre and film, MacMillan was of the same generation as John Osborne and other New Wave dramatists, and he admired their plays as a kindred spirit. Their gritty realism inspired the dark subject matter of his ballet *The Burrow* (1958), about refugees being hunted down by the secret police. He also worked as choreographer on Osborne's ill-starred musical, *The World of Paul Slickey* (1959), demonstrating a 'theatrical genius and originality' that made him Osborne's 'happiest and most valuable recruit'.

In the 1950s MacMillan formed two enduring partnerships. His long-term collaboration with Greek-born Nicholas Georgiadis as stage designer resulted in a series of outstanding and innovative works for several ballets. Meanwhile, Canadian dancer Lynn Seymour, whom MacMillan picked out from the *corps de ballet* to star in *The Burrow*, became his choreographic 'muse', inspiring many of the finest roles in his ballets over the next twenty years. Dame Ninette de Valois described her as the Royal Ballet's 'greatest dramatic dancer'. MacMillan found her deeply responsive to music:

> I can set a step to music and she will say, 'Why don't we do it this way on the music?' in a totally different manner. She can play around with music. She feels it so much in her body and through her body. I just have to say, 'Go in that direction' and she goes. I don't mean just physically, but mentally as well. She is so receptive, and she has a divine body; the instrument is truly wonderful.

Among MacMillan's most controversial works was *The Invitation* (1960), with Lynn Seymour as an innocent girl who is raped by the husband of an unhappily married couple. The daring subject matter, so compellingly danced, shocked traditionalists, made headlines and caused performances in schools to be banned. Both dancer and choreographer, however, were as determined as ever to stretch the language of dance in order to touch a deeper reality. As Lynn Seymour later observed, '[Kenneth] is not, nor am I, interested in imposing a glossy, beautiful shell on stage: truth of feeling is more important … The important thing is that the dance must be human; it can be ugly, odd, unexpected: that is what people are like.'

Their refusal to gloss over the darker side of human behaviour intensified the emotional and dramatic effect – qualities which some felt British ballet had lacked. In his book *Roland Petit* (1953), Peter Craig-Raymond argued that the English had trapped dance and drama into the 'drawing room':

> Anarchy may be the French substitute for the English submissiveness to technique and technique's discipline. But correct though it is, today's English ballet is a cold, conventional, *theatre-less* exercise … Puritanism, it may well be, still exists. The English, once working in an art form, seem to have a reactionary urge to get it out of its attic or theatre and into the drawing room. The drawing room whispers which dominate our plays and playwrights seem to bear this out.

Roland Petit was the *enfant terrible* of French ballet, who intrigued the English with his bold, theatrical choreography and avant-garde music and design. Petit's *chic* young company visited London six times in the 1950s, and included Violette Verdy, Renée Jeanmaire and Colette Marchand - famed as 'Les Legs'. In 1948 Margot Fonteyn had danced with Petit in Paris in *Les Demoiselles de la Nuit*, the ballet he created for her during their passionate affair. Petit's Ballets de Paris loved shocking audiences with music, steps and lighting effects centred on strong narratives with sexy, theatrical content and gesture drawn from everyday life. He worked with leading artists, composers and writers such as Derain, Berard, Cocteau, Anouilh, Milhaud and Orson Welles. In 1956 he presented at the Palace Theatre his celebrated ballets *Le Loup*, about a young bride's fatal love for a wolf, *Carmen* and *La Chambre*, with a libretto by the popular French detective novelist Georges Simenon, with music by Georges Auric and designs by Bernard Buffet.

The year 1956 also saw in London a 'Spanish Invasion', starting with Antonio and his Spanish Ballet Company at the Palace Theatre in September, followed by

Luisillo's Spanish Theatre Company at the Prince's, and Jose Greco at the Festival Hall. The same venue hosted Ram Gopal's Indian Ballet in *The Legend of the Taj Mahal* shortly after its success at the Edinburgh Festival. Gopal, who had tirelessly promoted Indian dance in Britain since 1939, appeared in this, his first full-length work.

By far the biggest sensation, however, was the Bolshoi Ballet's first visit to Covent Garden in October 1956. During the Cold War, a visit by a company from the Soviet Union was very rare, and competition for seats was fierce. Over a thousand people camped out for days in advance of the date when the tickets went on sale, the hottest tickets being those for Galina Ulanova in *Giselle* and *Romeo and Juliet*. A reciprocal visit by the Sadler's Wells Ballet to Russia in 1956 was cancelled due to the crisis provoked by the Soviet invasion of Hungary. Just a few years later, in 1961, Rudolf Nureyev's dramatic defection to the West made him an overnight celebrity. By 1962 he had forged an exciting professional relationship with the Royal Ballet, including a now legendary partnership with prima ballerina Margot Fonteyn.

A pioneer of American modern dance, Martha Graham and her company were first seen in Britain in 1954, where their performances were met with critical incomprehension and audience apathy. Championed only by the dance critic Richard Buckle in *The Observer*, her company did not return to Britain until 1963. In the intervening years, attitudes to modern dance had undergone a complete sea-change. For example, it was also in 1963 that Western Theatre Ballet, an innovative small-scale British ballet company, had a major success with Peter Darrell's short ballet *Mods and Rockers*, set to music by The Beatles. Graham's work was seen before large and enthusiastic audiences, and its impact eventually led to the formation of the London Contemporary Dance School in 1966 and the London Contemporary Dance Theatre in 1967 under the guidance of former Graham dancer Robert Cohan.

41 *The Invitation*
Lynn Seymour as the Young Girl and Desmond Doyle as the Husband, The Royal Ballet, Royal Opera House, Covent Garden, 1960
Photograph by Houston Rogers

The Invitation shocked its first audiences, prompting Oleg Kerensky to write in the *Daily Mail*, 'With its realistic rape scene and adult story, of two ultra-sensitive young innocents violated by an older and rather sinister couple, it could well be called an X-certificate ballet.'

42 *La Chambre*
Buzz Miller and Veronika Mlakar, Les Ballets de Paris de Roland Petit, Palace Theatre, London, 1956
Photograph by Houston Rogers

Roland Petit's 1955 ballet *La Chambre* received its London première on the same evening as the first performance of *Look Back in Anger*. Dealing with a murder reconstruction in a sleazy hotel room, the ballet was described by the dance critic A.V. Coton as amounting to 'a display of acrobatic-erotic dancing that would not have come amiss in the Colosseum (Rome) AD100.'

43 Antonio
1964
Photograph by
Anthony Crickmay

To audiences of the
1950s, Antonio and
Spanish dancing were
synonymous. Born in
Seville in 1921, he
began dancing as a
small child for coins in
the street. Before
Antonio, the best known
Spanish dancers in the
twentieth century were
women. His astonishing
pyrotechnics,
glamorous personality
and undeniable star
quality restored male
supremacy to Spanish
dance. His *zapateado*
(footwork) was
unbelievably fast, and
he was especially
famous for his
rhythmically complex
heel beats (*taconeo*),
which were so
remarkable that they
were recorded on disc.

44 Ram Gopal
1959
Photograph by
Houston Rogers

Ram Gopal popularised
classical Indian dance
throughout Europe,
America and Russia in
the mid-twentieth
century and was
nicknamed 'the Indian
Nijinsky'. His greatest
success was at the
1956 Edinburgh
Festival, when he
brought sixteen Indian
dancers to Scotland
and scored an artistic
triumph.

45 *Giselle*
Galina Ulanova as Giselle and Nikolai Fadeyechev as Albrecht with the Bolshoi Ballet at the Royal Opera House, Covent Garden, 1956
Photograph by Houston Rogers

The 1956 Bolshoi season was a sensation for London audiences, who thrilled at the dramatic intensity and technical virtuosity of dancers in a repertoire of (then) unfamiliar blockbusters, such as *Romeo and Juliet* and *The Fountain of Bakhchisarai*, and popular classics such as *Giselle* and *Swan Lake*.

46 *The Fountain of Bakhchisarai*
The male dancers of the Bolshoi Ballet on their 1956 British tour
Photograph by Houston Rogers

48 Night Journey
Martha Graham as
Jocasta, Edinburgh
Festival, 1963
Photograph by
Anthony Crickmay

47 The Sleeping Beauty
Nadia Nerina and
Rudolf Nureyev on the
cover of TV Times,
17–23 June 1962
Photograph by
Houston Rogers

In 1962 Nureyev
danced with several
leading ballerinas with
the Royal Ballet, on
stage and on television,
including Nadia Nerina.
The excitement of his
dancing and his
glamorous appeal
helped to make ballet a
popular mass-media
entertainment.

49 *Mods and Rockers*
Western Theatre Ballet,
Prince Charles
Theatre, London, 1963
Photograph by
Anthony Crickmay

Mods and Rockers was popular with fashionable young people. Dance critic Mary Clarke noted at one performance that 'There was a lot of leather in the audience the night I was there and no disapproval of what went on on the stage ... it is just honest-to-goodness pop, and I do not think that anyone who enjoys, say, the *Ready, Steady, Go* programme on television ... could resist it.'

50 *Mods and Rockers*
Gary Sherwood and
Deirdre O'Donohoe,
Western Theatre Ballet,
Yvonne Arnaud Theatre,
Guildford, 1965
Photograph by
Anthony Crickmay

Lonnie Donegan,
1956, Photograph by
Harry Hammond

'The film [Rock Around The Clock] was stopped for eighteen minutes, in the hope that the uproar among the audience of 900 would subside, but each time one of the "rock and roll" bands interrupted the story of the film with the first manic whine of the saxophone, boys leapt from the front stalls into the front aisle and stamped their suede shoes in the octopus whirling of jive.'

SCENE IN THE ODEON DESCRIBED IN THE
MANCHESTER GUARDIAN, 10 SEPTEMBER 1956

6 Stars in Their Eyes

Post-war London saw a boom in American musicals starting with *Oklahoma!* and *Annie Get Your Gun* in 1947. It continued with *Carousel, Kiss Me Kate, South Pacific, Paint Your Wagon, Guys and Dolls, The King and I, Pal Joey, Kismet,* peaked in 1958 with *My Fair Lady* and *West Side Story*, and lasted to the mid-1960s. Britain more than held its own against the American intruders with hits such as *Bless the Bride* (1947) by A.P. Herbert and Vivian Ellis, Sandy Wilson's *The Boy Friend* (1953–54), and *Salad Days* by Julian Slade and Dorothy Reynolds (1954). Despite their popularity in England, only one of these shows transferred to Broadway – *The Boy Friend*, in which Julie Andrews made her name. She went on to star in *My Fair Lady, Camelot* and, most famously, *The Sound of Music*.

The Boy Friend was set in a finishing school for young ladies in Nice in 1926. Its celebration of the flapper era was Sandy Wilson's 'valentine from one post-war period to another'. *Salad Days* was also about young people – students about to leave university for 'worthwhile' careers and social conformity, whose adventures involve Minnie a magic piano that makes everyone dance, and an uncle who travels by flying saucer.

Salad Days (2,283 performances) and *The Boy Friend* (2,084 performances) eventually joined the elite of long-running British musicals. Maybe they were a soothing alternative to what *The Times* called 'the hard-hitting, hard-boiled American musical'. Reviewing Brecht's *Threepenny Opera* in 1956, Milton Shulman complained that 'niceness' was a selling point for British musicals, but represented 'a retreat into simpering wholesomeness'.

Meanwhile *West Side Story*, which began its London run of 1,040 performances in December 1958, was pushing the American musical to the limits with teenage youth embroiled in gang rivalry and racial conflict. The territory is a New York street; the 'adult' world is reduced to a backdrop, and its 'authority figures' get scant respect. The Jets, a motley gang of native-born Americans, fight to keep their street territory from the Sharks, a gang of recently arrived Puerto Ricans. Leonard Bernstein's score and Jerome Robbins' sensational choreography created a young persons' world of restless energy. The outstanding cast featured the young, rather than old Broadway names, and young fans championed the show and its songs. It expressed a dark side of American youth culture that paralleled Britain's rival gangs of teddy boys, mods versus rockers, and the Notting Hill race riots of August 1958.

British musicals showed more inclination to 'realism' later in the 1950s, and discovered a major native talent in Lionel Bart, whose songs for Cliff Richard's first number-one hit ('Livin' Doll'), Frank Norman's play *Fings Ain't Wot They Used T'Be* and *Lock Up Your Daughters* at the Mermaid Theatre presaged his smash-hit *Oliver!* in 1960. Wolf Mankovitz and Julian More featured low-life Soho in *Expresso Bongo* (1958), said to be based on Bermondsey-born Tommy Hicks, who was a sailor before he become the pop star Tommy Steele with 'Singing the Blues'. He later starred in *Half a Sixpence* (1963), adapted from H.G. Wells's *Kipps* by David Heneker, which became a hit in both London and New York.

Britain's first hit chart, published in 1952 in the *New Musical Express*, encouraged American vocalists and bands to appear in the UK. Touring the theatre circuit boosted sales of their records and songs, which London's 'Tin Pan Alley' published in vast numbers. An added attraction was top billing on *Sunday Night at the London Palladium*, which ATV broadcast live to the nation from 1955 to 1972, followed by a tour. Cardiff-born Shirley Bassey made her television début at the Palladium in 1957, the year of her first hit, 'The Banana Boat Song'. Buddy Holly's British tour in 1958 inspired the future Beatles. Elvis Presley never performed in the UK, but did set foot on Scottish soil *en route* for the USA in 1960.

American rock crossed the Atlantic via such films as *The Blackboard Jungle*, which was released in Britain in October 1955, six months before *Rebel Without a Cause* starring James Dean. *The Blackboard Jungle* showed young fans jiving to Bill Haley and his Comets' performance of 'Rock around the Clock', which soon topped the British charts. Ironically, Haley's tour of Britain was to flop in 1957 because in the flesh he appeared too old to young audiences (he was thirty).

Lonnie Donegan, playing in Chris Barber's Jazz Band, recorded 'Rock Island Line' in November 1954. A speeded-up version of an old Lead Belly blues number, it helped to popularise skiffle. When Decca, noting the impact of Bill Haley, issued it as a ten-inch single a year later, it leapt to No.1 in January 1956. Inspired by Black American music, skiffle gave teenagers their own music for the first time. It could be played 'any old how', with just two cheap guitars, a washboard for rhythm, and a broom handle, piece of string and tea chest for the bass. John Lennon with his Quarrymen were performing skiffle at a fête in 1957 when he met Paul McCartney. Like George Harrison, Paul belonged to the local Lonnie Donegan

Skiffle Club. Many groups graduated from skiffle to rock 'n' roll or folk.

Students and Angry Young Men such as Jimmy Porter in *Look Back in Anger* regarded rock as juvenile and working-class. They preferred traditional jazz, based on New Orleans jazz, played by Chris Barber, George Melly and Humphrey Lyttleton in the latter's club at 100 Oxford Street. Burgeoning interest in the new music forced BBC TV to launch *6.5 Special* in 1957, a precursor of today's *Top of the Pops*; ABC Television created a rival show, *Oh Boy!*, in 1958.

Groups mushroomed across the country. Liverpool, which had more than 300 venues, produced The Beatles, The Searchers, Gerry and the Pacemakers, and even evolved its own bright, metallic 'Mersey Sound'. Although Britain and Europe were gripped by Beatlemania in 1963, The Beatles' records were not selling well in the USA, which was a notorious graveyard for visiting British artists. The breakthrough came in October when Ed Sullivan saw screaming Beatles fans at Heathrow and invited the group to appear on his American television show.

The Beatles' arrival at John F. Kennedy airport on 7 February 1964, their performances in New York's Carnegie Hall, and appearance on Ed Sullivan's show – seen by 73 million Americans – began the 'The British Invasion' of the USA. By the end of March The Beatles occupied the top five slots in the American charts. Back home, the Top Ten of the UK's hit parade on 14 March was all-British for the first time ever, and Radio Caroline, Britain's first pirate radio station, began transmitting rock and pop around the clock.

51 *Salad Days*
Sheila Chester as Jane in the touring production, 1960
Photograph by Houston Rogers

Salad Days was written to fill a three-week gap in the summer season at the Bristol Old Vic in 1954. Julian Slade, the musical director and composer at the

theatre, joined with actress Dorothy Reynolds to write this gentle, frivolous tale of a magic piano. The show took on a life of its own, transferred to London and eventually outran even *Oklahoma!* in a staggering five-and-a-half-year run at the traditionally unlucky Vaudeville Theatre.

52 *West Side Story*
Her Majesty's Theatre, London, 1959
Photograph by Angus McBean

Devised by choreographer Jerome Robbins, *West Side Story* was an adaptation of *Romeo and Juliet* in which the rival families of Montague and

Capulet were translated into the warring gangs of New York's West Side. While critics of *Salad Days* made slighting comparisons with vicarage tea parties, *West Side Story* lent itself to articles in the press on 'Does stage violence really have so serious an effect on children?'

53 Ray Martin and Monty Norman in the first self-service listening booth in a record shop, *1954*
Photograph by Harry Hammond

54 Cliff Richard
The first time he appeared as the 'top of the bill', Chiswick Empire, London, 1958
Photograph by Harry Hammond

In 1958 Harry Webb changed his name to Cliff Richard and started a band, The Drifters, who played in pubs and clubs. By the end of that year, their single 'Move It' had reached number two in the charts, and Cliff embarked on what was to become one of the longest careers in pop history.

55 Shirley Bassey
*making her TV début
'live' at the London
Palladium
1957
Photograph by
Harry Hammond*

Shirley Bassey had
been working in a
sausage factory and
singing in working
men's clubs in her
native town of Cardiff,
when in 1955 she was
discovered by Jack
Hylton. Her powerful
voice and stage
presence soon
established her as
a star in Britain and
America.

**56 Cliff Richard and
the Shadows on the set
of the film *Expresso
Bongo*, 1958**
*Photograph by
Harry Hammond*

Expresso Bongo was an
extremely popular stage
musical, which played at
the Saville Theatre,
London, in 1958. Called
the 'Angry Young
Musical', the show
sharply satirised the pop
business of the late
1950s. The original cast
included Paul Scofield,
James Kenney, Millicent
Martin and Barry Cryer. It
was awarded the London
Critics' Award for Best
Musical 1957–58 and
was quickly made into a
film starring Laurence
Harvey and Cliff
Richard. The film's
choreography was
created by Kenneth
MacMillan.

58 Lonnie Donegan
1956
Photograph by
Harry Hammond

Glasgow-born Lonnie
Donegan helped launch
the skiffle movement in
Britain. His 'anyone
can do it' attitude and
popular appeal inspired
many bands and
singers, including the
future Beatles. Between
1958 and 1962 he had
thirty-one top 30 UK
hits, and was a favourite
on TV pop shows, such
as *Oh Boy!* and the
6.5 Special.

57 Elvis Presley
1960
Photograph by
Harry Hammond

Harry Hammond
managed to photograph
Elvis Presley on the
only occasion he set
foot on British soil.
Elvis was on his way
home to America in
1960, after serving
his two-year US Army
conscription in
Germany. On the
stopover at Prestwick
Airport, Glasgow, he
gave a press
conference.

59 Jazz at the Royal Albert Hall
1954
Photograph by
Harry Hammond

60 *6.5 Special*
BBC TV show, 1958
Photograph by
Harry Hammond

In 1957 the BBC decided to try to attract the growing teenage television audience, and devised the popular magazine programme *6.5 Special* (so named because it was broadcast at 6.05pm on Saturdays). Produced by Josephine Douglas and Jack Good, *6.5 Special* featured rock 'n' roll stars such as Tommy Steele, jazz artists such as Johnny Dankworth and Humphrey Lyttleton, and the skiffle of Lonnie Donegan.

61 Tommy Steele and the Dallas Boys
performing on the Oh Boy! *TV show, 1958*
Photograph by Harry Hammond

Tommy Steele was touted as a British Elvis Presley in the late 1950s, and by 1961 he had had eighteen hit singles. In a career change in 1962 he appeared as Tony Lumpkin in *She Stoops to Conquer* at the Old Vic, followed in 1963 by the long-running stage musical *Half a Sixpence*.

62 *King Kong*
Prince's Theatre,
London, 1960
Photograph by
Houston Rogers

King Kong, a South African
'jazz opera', told the
downbeat tale of a black
boxer felled by his own
foolish brutishness. The
show's exuberant dancing
and 'novelty value' kept it
running at the Prince's
Theatre for six months.
During the 1950s and early
1960s, several popular black
musical shows were
performed in London,
including *Porgy and Bess*
and *Black Nativity*.

63 Helen Shapiro
1961
Photograph by
Harry Hammond

Helen Shapiro had her
first hit, 'Don't Treat Me
Like A Child', in 1961,
when she was only
fourteen years old. The
public were astonished
by her mature-sounding
voice, and she quickly
followed her initial
success with two
number-one records,
including her best-
known song, 'Walking
Back to Happiness'.

64 The Beatles
1963
Photograph by
Harry Hammond

This photograph was taken just after Ringo Starr joined the band. That year The Beatles made their second single and their first album, both called *Please Please Me.* The album stayed at number one in the charts for twenty-nine weeks. By 1963 they were setting the trend in clothes, haircuts and music all over Europe. By 1964 they had conquered America and were on their way to being the most successful and influential band of the twentieth century.

Harold Pinter
c.1960

'The actor then found that to communicate his invisible meanings [without words] he needed concentration, he needed will; he needed to summon all his emotional reserves; he needed courage; he needed clear thought. But the most important result was that he was led inexorably to the conclusion that he needed form.'

PETER BROOK, *THE EMRTY SPACE* (1968)

7 Invisible Meanings

Brought up in London's East End, Harold Pinter is no stranger to anti-Semitism; threat, menace and insecurity are central to his work. His early years as an actor included touring in the provinces with Anew McMaster and Donald Wolfit before, in 1957, he wrote *The Room* and *The Birthday Party*. Pinter sent *The Birthday Party* to Peter Hall after seeing his production of *Waiting for Godot* (see chapter 3), but Hall couldn't take it on.

Michael Codron first produced *The Birthday Party* with Peter Wood directing a strong cast that included Beatrix Lehmann and John Slater at the Arts Theatre, Cambridge, in April 1958. According to local reviews, the first-night audience 'warmly received' the play, giving it a 'great ovation'. But in London three weeks later the daily press were so negative that it ran for only a week. Milton Shulman attacked its 'irreverent verbal anarchy' and attempts to make 'the futility of language' funny, while the *Manchester Guardian* hated the mystification: 'What all this means, only Mr Pinter knows, for as his characters speak in non-sequiturs, half-gibberish and lunatic ravings, they are unable to explain their actions, thoughts, or feelings. If the author can forget Beckett, Ionesco, and Simpson, he may do much better next time.' Harold Hobson mounted a stout defence in *The Sunday Times*, but it was too late to save the production.

The hard line of the national dailies at the London première contrasts with the initial reaction at Cambridge Arts. One reviewer there found the puzzling plot a small price to pay for Pinter's 'masterly' dialogue, which showed that 'English drama is at last getting out of its rut.' The same reviewer described how the dramatic mood shifts from Meg and Petey's opening exchanges – as ordinary as the sauce bottles on the table – to Stanley's insecure outbursts; and how the 'frightening rhythm' of his drumming anticipates Goldberg and McCann's interrogation, which reaches a 'climax of sadism'. The reviewer sensed how the dramatic language generates feeling that shapes the play as a whole. Pinter once discussed with Samuel Beckett how form relates to feeling. Beckett observed: 'If you insist on finding form, I'll describe it for you … I was in hospital once. There was a man in another ward, dying of throat cancer. In the silence, I could hear his screams continually. That's the only kind of form my work has.'

Peter Hall, who has since directed a dozen of Pinter's premières, respects his linguistic rhythms as meticulously as he does Shakespeare's or Beckett's. Hall instinctively knows how long the famous Pinter 'silences' and 'pauses' should be, and how he chooses words with a poet's precision: 'Pinter's words are weapons that the characters use to discomfort or destroy each other; and, in defence, to conceal feelings.' *The Birthday Party* was the first of Pinter's plays to be staged in America; it achieved classic status with the Royal Shakespeare Company's 1964 Aldwych revival.

The year 1964 was highly important for the RSC. Its celebrations of the 400th anniversary of Shakespeare's birth coincided with its most adventurous contemporary work. The urge to discover new theatrical expression came to a head in Peter Brook's 'Theatre of Cruelty' season at LAMDA (London Academy of Music and Dramatic Art). With Charles Marowitz, Brook formed an experimental group to find a 'common language' that could open up new possibilities for actors and directors.

Marowitz had assisted Brook on his nihilistic 1962 production of *King Lear* for the RSC. 'Theatre of Cruelty' took inspiration from the French director Antonin Artaud's idea of a 'cruel theatre' that exalted violent ritual and images above words. Brook used the group to break down old theatrical forms such as 'story', 'construction', 'rounded characters', ingrown naturalistic techniques and bourgeois taboos. Above all he wanted to discover a modern equivalent to Shakespearian blank verse that would make 'a contemporary theatre event as bold and dense as an Elizabethan event could be'.

The group was given texts to explore and rehearse before an audience. The 'surrealistic vaudeville' included extracts from Jarry's *Ubu Roi*; Artaud's only work in dialogue form, *The Spurt of Blood*; Marowitz's deconstructed *Hamlet*; a sketch featuring Jackie Kennedy and Christine Keeler as fellow victims of media obsession; exercises involving white masks; a graphic description of the plague in 1500; and a short story 'Scene' by Alain Robbe-Grillet. Some pieces called for spectacular effects. Artaud's, for instance, featured a giant hand of God whose bitten wrist flooded the stage in blood, and a prostitute whose lifted skirts revealed a nest of scorpions. This required inspired design input from Sally Jacobs and initiated her twenty-year working relationship with Brook.

The 'Theatre of Cruelty' season helped to establish an ensemble open to fresh ideas and techniques in productions that followed, such as the *Marat/Sade*. Peter Weiss, a Czech-born Swedish artist, director and writer, based his play, whose full title is *The Persecution and Assassination of Marat as Performed by the Inmates of the Asylum of Charenton under the Direction of the Marquis de Sade*, on a slender fact. In 1808 the Marquis de Sade got inmates to re-enact in the bath-house of their asylum the murder of Marat, a leader of the French Revolution, fifteen years earlier.

The production drew on the best theatrical ingredients of the day: Brechtian, didactic, absurdist non-text-based 'happenings' in the USA, and Artaud. Designer Sally Jacobs described the production thus: 'Marat and de Sade discuss the nature of man and the nature of revolution. The Inmates, led by a Herald and four Clowns, play out these themes in many, and varied musical set pieces; and except when they close themselves into the baths, the Inmates are present throughout – a unique aspect of Peter Brook's work at that time.'

Although it was a triumph of 'total theatre' in which every element played a vital role, special credit must be given to Sally Jacobs' brilliant set. Michael Hallifax recalls how the audience was 'faced with a totally grey stage – grey wooden, steeply raked flooring and a grey surround … The skilfulness of the setting was not apparent immediately to the audience until a scene change, which demanded the stage to be full one moment and empty the next. This Sally Jacobs achieved by having the stage floor honeycombed with traps.'

Violent and controversial, the *Marat/Sade* was a radical departure for the RSC that initiated a heated media debate about the direction that the theatre in general, and the RSC in particular, were taking. It had a visceral impact worthy of Artaud, and caused a major row when Sir Emile Littler, a member of the RSC's Executive Council, publicly dissociated himself from 'the programmes of dirt plays at the Aldwych'. On the other hand it bowled over critics like Bernard Levin, who wrote that it was 'without doubt one of the half-dozen most amazing achievements in *mise-en-scène* that the English theatre has seen in my lifetime'.

65 *The Caretaker*
by Harold Pinter
Arthur Pentelow as
Davies and Stephen
MacDonald as Aston,
Birmingham Repertory
Theatre, 1961
Photograph by
Lisel Haas

66 *The Birthday Party*
Beatrix Lehmann as
Meg and John Slater
as Goldberg, Lyric
Theatre, Hammersmith,
1958

The *Sunday Times* critic Harold Hobson, who missed the opening night but attended the Thursday matinée in an audience of seven, including the playwright, reacted very differently from most to the play's absurdist uncertainties. He wrote that Pinter was 'the most original, disturbing, and arresting talent in theatrical London'. By the time his review came out, however, the Lyric had taken the play off.

Specially photographed for " THE SKETCH " by Houston Rogers.

THE BROOKS OFF-STAGE

Mr. and Mrs. Peter Brook both come of Russian stock and they share a taste for music : the piano is an important furnishing of their Kensington home. Since leaving Oxford, he has been responsible for a number of distinguished and sometimes controversial productions ; his Covent Garden and Stratford seasons will be long remembered, but for different reasons, and his film, *The Beggar's Opera*, made a fresh and exciting use of colour and movement. Mrs. Brook is, in public life, Natasha Parry, who may be seen on the stage in *Charley's Aunt* at the Strand Theatre, on the screen in *Knave of Hearts* at the Ritz Cinema. His production of *The Dark is Light Enough* at the Aldwych Theatre (happily next door to the Strand) has been praised, and a further production (of Arthur Macrae's new comedy, *Both Ends Meet*) will open at the Apollo Theatre on June 9th. After that, when Mrs. Brook is free, they plan a long holiday.

67 Peter Brook with his wife, the actress Natasha Parry, 1954
Photograph by Houston Rogers

68 The Theatre of Cruelty season
Programme cover for the Royal Shakespeare Company at the LAMDA Theatre, London, 1964

The Theatre of Cruelty was a theory of theatre developed by Antonin Artaud in the 1930s. It was characterised by intensity of performance and extremity of action, gesture and physical expression. It sought to shock the audience into recognising man's inherent brutishness when free of the restrictions of conventional social behaviour.

69 *Ubu Roi*
Costume designs by
Sally Jacobs, 1964
Ubu (left) and Ma Ubu

Ma UBU – [UBU ROI]
Theatre of Cruelty 1964
Sally Jacobs

70 *Marat/Sade*
Newspaper articles from the
London Evening News *and*
Daily Mail, *1964*

WEST END THEATRE STORM GROWS

One of the most amazing plays I've ever seen

Emile Littler Joins Protest

By BILL BOORNE

FIERCE criticism of many of the plays now being performed by the Royal Shakespeare Company during th...

THEATRE'S VIEW OF VIOLENCE

An open discussion called "Violence —Private and Public", was held at the Aldwych Theatre last night by the Royal Shakespeare Theatre Club. The context was Mr. Peter Weiss's play *The Marat/...*

...which opened here last week.

We...
D...
Thi...

WHAT ab...
stage to...
Send y...
Editor ...
News.
There ...
for each ...
and two ...
theatre (...

...Assassination of Marat ... Peter Weiss. Royal ...e Company, Aldwych ... Theatre

...traordinary play ...s with an acorn ...that when the

By BERNARD LEVIN

Ambitious Example of Theatre of Cruelty

Aldwych Theatre: *The Persecution a...*

...ssassination of Marat as Performed by ...er the Direction of the Marquis de Sad...
...matic Critic

...leath, the cast

...Aldwych *by Gerard Fay*

And the murder is interrupted for a lightning review of the years that have passed from 1793 to 1808, ending with the lunatics singing:

...rching on
...l different
...ns.
...llions.

...is not so
...r although
...ramatically
...work, if the
...de Sade is

Sade is driving them up the wall

CHARLES GREVILLE

JUST watching one performance of the Royal Shakespeare Company's demented exercise in blood and lunacy known as *The Marat/Sade* is a harrowing enough experi-

cast is panting to finish with it all and come home in April.

Ian Richardson, who plays Marat, said in New York yesterday that "there is not a single member of the cast who does not hate with deep loathing every single per-

entire two hours of the play, admits that he is "hitting the bottle"—the only way he can unwind after the show. He ends every performance dripping with sweat, drained both emotionally and physically.

"Every evening it gets

...he theatre ...arge scale. ...which pro-...nternational ...try Peter ...ely named ...ssassination ...Inmates of ...e the Direc-...he opening ...r Brook, is ...ut once the ...c, a thriller, ...is the best ...don at the ...are nowa-...c terms like ...and lunatic ...ospitals. This ...madmen and ...nd is quite ...ere is a touch ...ge is more

peutic theatrical performances which de Sade produced under the free-minded, long pre-Freudian supervision of de Coulmier who ran the Charenton Bedlam. The play deals with the stabbing to death of Marat, in his bath, by Charlotte Corday. It is a bloodbath, violently attacking the emotions and sensibilities of any audience. It will send Aunt Edna round the bend but cannot fail to conquer anyone who has the slightest trace of compassion in him.

The story is acted out in a deadly insane charade which as it approaches moments of meaninglessness becomes most emphatic-ally true and moving. There seem to be, to begin with, many false notes but they all ring true in the end, even in the music which is anything but incidental. The acting? Nobody is merely a player, the smallest incidents are done with complete conviction but Clive Revill as Marat, Glenda Jackson as Corday, Ian Richardson as the Herald and Patrick Magee as de Sade all achieve performances which it ...uiding to call merely

71 *Marat/Sade*
Set model by Sally Jacobs, 1964
S.665-1986

Sally Jacobs' design involved an almost bare stage with drab brick walls. The central circle of wooden duckboards covers baths sunk into the floor. The holes at the front are drains, into which blood is poured and heads dropped during a re-enactment of the guillotine being used. Sally Jacobs was encouraged to continue experimenting throughout the rehearsal period, so the set could develop in line with the play.

72 *Marat/Sade*
The Royal Shakespeare
Company, Aldwych
Theatre, London, 1964
Photograph by
Morris Newcombe

Joan Plowright, 1959
Photograph by
Sandra Lousada

'In 1959 I was justifiably slotted into the "kitchen sink" category after the first night of Roots. I say "justifiably" only because there was a real sink on stage, not to mention a real stove on which liver and bacon were cooked. The play itself, however, was concerned with a great many other, and more weighty, matters. I am eternally indebted to Arnold Wesker, who provided for the contemporary actress what Osborne had provided for the actor – a character who spoke to and for our own generation and who had never before been seen on an English stage.'

JOAN PLOWRIGHT, *AND THAT'S NOT ALL* (2001)

8 Class Acts

Arnold Wesker was one of the leading working-class playwrights to emerge in the 1950s. The success of his early plays *Roots*, *Chips With Everything* and *The Kitchen* meant that he became associated with the promotion of 'kitchen-sink' drama. Around the same time, a young generation of actors from the regions was challenging the hegemony of the Home Counties and 'received pronunciation' in British theatre. Scunthorpe-born Joan Plowright proved herself a leading interpreter of New Wave drama in 1959 as Beatie Bryant in Wesker's *Roots*. In 1957 Plowright had played Jean Rice in *The Entertainer* (see chapter 4) opposite Laurence Olivier, whom she later married.

Roots was the second play in a trilogy by Wesker. It follows the fortunes of the Kahns, an East End Jewish family, from the anti-Semitism of the 1930s to the Hungarian revolution in 1956 and the contemporary disenchantment with post-war socialism. The first play, *Chicken Soup with Barley*, and the third, *I'm Talking About Jerusalem*, were based on Wesker's own East End experiences, while *Roots* drew on those of his wife's family, whom he met while working as a bookseller's assistant and kitchen porter in Norwich.

In its Norfolk setting, the dialogue of *Roots* has a strong regional flavour, like the Lancashire speech rhythms of Shelagh Delaney's *A Taste of Honey*. Beatie, who is on a flying visit home, has been living in London with Ronnie Kahn, a working-class intellectual. Ronnie's opinions – which Beatie loves to quote – are contrasted with those of the rural culture in which she grew up. When her family prepares a welcoming party for him, he fails to appear and ends his relationship with Beatie. Instead of parroting his views, she is compelled to find her own voice and personal freedom.

In 1961 Wesker became Director of Centre 42 theatre, based at the Roundhouse in Chalk Farm, London. With the backing of the trade union movement, it aimed to make the arts more accessible to all classes of people, but it was sadly short-lived. As Christopher Innes observed, Centre 42 enabled artists to control 'their own channels of distribution' and speak directly to a mass audience, so that the public could 'see that artistic activity is a natural part of their daily lives'. Instead of fostering mindless escapism, artists could apply a socialist vision that challenged the audience to ask questions, overcoming the barriers of education that divided them.

Another forthright exponent of the New Wave was Shelagh Delaney, who had worked in an engineering factory and as a photographer's assistant when she saw Terence Rattigan's play *Variation on a Theme* in Manchester. Convinced that she could do better, she wrote *A Taste of Honey* in a fortnight. Its title, inspired by the Bible, reflects her experience of love; its setting is contemporary Salford, her home town; and its eighteen-year-old anti-heroine Josephine is based on herself.

Delaney sent her script to Joan Littlewood at Stratford East, introducing herself as the 'English Françoise Sagan'. Littlewood radically reworked the text with the cast, and linked the scenes with live jazz. According to the programme, Shelagh Delaney was unlike London's Angry Young Men in knowing 'what she is angry about … coming from a Lancashire city which is devastated not by war but by industry and by years of pre-war unemployment'.

The *Times'* review is worth quoting:

> In outline the plot suggests a mood of interminable and squalid pathos: a prostitute abandons her adolescent daughter and marries; left alone, the girl has an affair with a West Indian who also makes off, leaving her pregnant; a forlorn art student moves in to take care of her, only to be driven off when the mother, her marriage in ruins, returns to restore the status quo. … Nothing could be less sentimental than Miss Delaney's treatment of these emotionally charged events.

The reviewer praised Delaney's 'great respect for northern speech … and how the language almost determines the play's atmosphere'. The *Observer* detected a 'smell of living' that challenged the audience: 'When the theatre presents poor people as good, we call it "sentimental." When it presents them as bad, we sniff and cry "squalid." Happily, Miss Delaney does not yet know about us and our squeamishness, which we think moral but which is really social. She is too busy recording the wonder of life as she lives it.' The *Daily Mail*, on the other hand, observed that Angry Young Women were even worse than Angry Young Men, found the Lancashire accents and direct address too much like music hall, and concluded that 'once, authors wrote good plays set in drawing-rooms. Now, under the Welfare State, they write bad plays set in garrets'.

Delaney's unsentimental handling of female sexuality, illegitimacy and other issues in *A Taste of Honey* reflects a working-class resilience and mental toughness. According to the programme, her 'fierce independence' and 'integrity of mind' made her 'typical of many of today's young people in the North of England'. She was thus of her time yet ahead of her time in other respects, such as portraying a gay character on stage and opting for a life without men. Unfortunately, her next play, *The Lion in Love*, was rejected by Joan Littlewood and savaged by the press when the Royal Court staged it in 1960. John Osborne was disgusted at the critics' treatment of the talented twenty-year-old: 'it was a classic example of a second play being demolished on the grounds of feigned admiration of the first. None of the women playwrights who followed Shelagh possessed a fraction of her four-square plain gifts and poetic realism.'

While directing a wealth of new work at Stratford East, Joan Littlewood staged productions of classic plays such as *Edward II* and *The Country Wife*, and important American dramas such as Tennessee Williams' *The Glass Menagerie*, in which she also appeared. Her 'reworking' of scripts was legendary, as Frank Norman discovered when she directed his *Fings Ain't Wot They Used T'Be* – a hit for Theatre Workshop in 1959. Although he had written it as a straight play, she decided it needed songs and, without consulting Norman, asked Lionel Bart to compose music and lyrics. During rehearsals the cast improvised around the text or created new situations needing more songs. As another writer, Wolf Mankowitz, observed: 'Joan doesn't know what her intentions are until she acts them out on the stage.'

Created by Joan Littlewood and Theatre Workshop in 1963, *Oh! What a Lovely War* ruthlessly exposed the horrors of the trenches and the incompetence of the ruling classes that sent thousands of men to their deaths in the First World War. The show was dressed up as an Edwardian music-hall show performed by pierrots. As part of the creation process the company invited local Eastenders to come and see the work in progress, and eventually incorporated some of their stories into the production.

**73 Arnold Wesker
(right) with Diane
Cilento and Alan Bates,
1965**
*Photograph by
Anthony Crickmay*

74 *Roots*
*Joan Plowright as
Beatie, Royal Court,
London, 1959*
*Photograph by
Sandra Lousada*

The first production of
Roots was designed by
Jocelyn Herbert, who

said that 'It was the first
naturalistic play I'd
done and the problem
was to do it in a non-
heavy way, especially
since it had three sets. I
only had eighty pounds
to spend and we kept
within the budget, but I
remember we weren't

able to afford an
outside lavatory and a
clothes line that we
wanted and which would
have cost an extra five
pounds. The design was
a breakthrough in a way,
my first attempt at
poetic realism for a
naturalistic play.'

75 *A Taste of Honey*
Set designed by John Bury, Theatre Workshop, Theatre Royal, Stratford East, 1958
Photograph by David Sim

76 Shelagh Delaney
1958
Photograph by Houston Rogers

A working-class girl from Salford in Lancashire, Shelagh Delaney loved theatre but was bored by the blandness of plays by and about middle-class people. She also objected to the portrayal of people from the north of England as 'gormless'.

77 *A Taste of Honey*
Murray Melvin as Geoffrey and Frances Cuka as Josephine, Theatre Workshop, Theatre Royal, Stratford East, 1958
Photograph by David Sim

Shelagh Delaney originally began *A Taste of Honey* as a novel but quickly realised that it would work better as a play. In 1958 Joan Littlewood agreed to produce her play at Stratford East. The following year the play transferred to the West End to great acclaim, garnering the inevitable name tag of the 'Angry Young Woman' for its author. The critic and film director Lindsay Anderson called *A Taste of Honey* 'a work of complete, exhilarating originality'.

78 Joan Littlewood
Oil painting by
Margaret Nicholson,
1931
S.95-1986

Directed by Joan
Littlewood, Theatre
Workshop was created
by a group of actors
committed to a left-
wing ideology. They
devised and
commissioned plays by
and about the working
class in the UK and
experimented with
physical approaches to
characterisation,
inspired by the work of
Rudolf Laban. Many of
their actors came from
non-theatrical
backgrounds.
In 1953 Theatre
Workshop moved to the
derelict Theatre Royal
in Stratford East,
London. The actors

lived in the dressing
rooms and slowly
redecorated the theatre
between rehearsals.
Despite its commitment
to bringing a diverse
programme of work to
the local community, it
was only after
international
recognition that the

local council
considered funding the
theatre. Their
reworkings of *Volpone*
and *Arden of*
Faversham were
performed in Paris at
the International
Festival of Theatre in
1955 to much acclaim.

80 *Oh! What a*
Lovely War
Cover of the souvenir
programme, Theatre
Workshop, Wyndham's
Theatre, London, 1963

81 *Oh! What a*
Lovely War
Page from the souvenir
programme, showing
Avis Bunnage, Theatre
Workshop, Wyndham's
Theatre, London, 1963

79 *The Glass*
Menagerie
by Tennessee Williams

Joan Littlewood
as Amanda, Olive
McFarland as Laura
and Robin Chapman
as Tom, Theatre

Workshop, Theatre
Royal, Stratford
East, 1958
Photograph by
John Spinner

And on Saturday I'm willing,
if you'll only take the shilling,
to make a man of any one of you.
Avis Bunnage

82 (below) *Fings Ain't Wot They Used T'Be*
Theatre Workshop, Theatre Royal, Stratford East, 1959
Photograph by Jeff Vickers

Frank Norman was able to draw on his extensive knowledge of the London criminal underworld for his play about a razor gang and a gambling house, while Lionel Bart provided the songs. The original cast included Barbara Windsor, Youtha Joyce and Toni Palmer, with a cameo appearance by Shelagh Delaney. The play raised concerns about where kitchen sink realism was heading. The two years Norman had spent in prison for fraud and his familiarity with Soho lent cachet and authenticity to the plot. But was it appropriate to sing and joke about living members of the demi-monde, exposing their world to the gaze of playgoers?

83 (above) *Fings Ain't Wot They Used T'Be*
Barbara Windsor as Rosie and Toni Palmer as Betty, Theatre Workshop, Theatre Royal, Stratford East, 1959
Photograph by Jeff Vickers

84 Lionel Bart and Alma Cogan, 1959
Photograph by Harry Hammond

Lionel Bart was a child when a teacher told his parents that he was a musical genius. He was given a violin to play, but he didn't practise and the lessons stopped. As a young man he joined the Communist Party and wrote the lyrics for an agit-prop version of *Cinderella* at the Unity Theatre. Bart then embarked on a career as a composer of pop songs. He chalked up hits for Cliff Richard and Tommy Steele before going on to compose the popular musicals *Fings Ain't Wot They Used T'Be* and *Oliver!* This photograph shows Bart with the pop star Alma Cogan, 'the girl with a laugh in her voice', who made her stage début singing in the chorus of *High Button Shoes* with the then unknown Audrey Hepburn.

Earle Hyman and
Soraya Rafat, 1958
Photograph by
Angus McBean

'What were they thinking, these 492 men from Jamaica and Trinidad, as the Empire Windrush slid upstream with the flood between the closing shores of Kent and Essex? ... And what has made them leave Jamaica?... They spoke independently, but unanimously, of a blight that has come upon the West Indies since those who have served America and Britain during the war returned home. The cost of living is high, wages are low. Many can earn no wages ...'

IAIN HAMILTON, 'WHY 492 WEST INDIANS CAME TO BRITAIN', *MANCHESTER GUARDIAN* (23 JUNE 1948)

9 Promised Land

The post-war era saw a shortage of labour in the UK and recession in the West Indies. From 1948 to 1962 anyone from British colonies or protectorates could register as British nationals under the British Nationality Act 1948. Between 1953 and 1955, when the US tightened up its entry restrictions, the number of immigrants entering the UK quadrupled. Around 160,000 West Indians and more than 50,000 migrants from India and Pakistan came to live in Britain between 1955 and 1960.

The English Stage Company at the Royal Court was the first to stage Caribbean writing in London. In 1958 it produced Barry Reckord's *Flesh to a Tiger* and Errol John's *Moon on a Rainbow Shawl*. Jamaican-born Barry Reckord won a scholarship to Emmanuel College, Cambridge, and wrote *Della* while reading English there. After he returned to Jamaica to teach, a friend sent the script to the Royal Court. Tony Richardson agreed to direct it but changed the title to *Flesh to a Tiger*. The Royal Court went on to stage several of his works, notably *Skyvers* (1963), about pupils in a London secondary modern school.

Della, the lead character in *Flesh to a Tiger*, is poor and unemployed, like the others in the Jamaican slum who come to the 'balm yard' to sing, dance and work magic on their enemies. They are led by a 'Shepherd' whose sect, outwardly Christian, promotes voodoo and superstition. Thwarted in his desire for Della, the Shepherd tells her that her baby will die, when it is actually being kept alive by a white doctor whom Della finds attractive, despite her neighbour's warning that 'black to white is flesh to a tiger; when they cross it, they tear it'. But the white doctor both desires and demeans her, and she rejects him and his race. Trapped between white domination and religious superstition, she smothers her baby to pin the blame on the Shepherd. When this fails she kills him.

Reckord believed the Royal Court took the play on because 'it was exotic and the language was poetic and this is what they expect from black people' (interview for *Blackgrounds*, 22 April 1997). Richardson recalled that the play was of clumsy construction, but had 'a passion of language which was extraordinary, especially in its evocation of the brutalities of slavery'. The inexperienced cast found the play intimidating yet 'wonderfully worthwhile'. With designer Loudon Sainthill's setting of rags and canes, 'reeking of sensuousness and decay', the production was highly atmospheric, with sound effects ranging from bird-calls to rituals with live goats.

Richardson's support for black practitioners dated back to the early 1950s, when he cast Gordon Heath, a black American folk-singer, as the first black Othello to be seen in a BBC television production. Richardson's view that, given the scarcity of black roles, a white actor playing Othello was a travesty was ahead of its time and did not begin to prevail until the 1980s. His experience of *Flesh to a Tiger* may have inspired Richardson to invite Paul Robeson to play the narrator Gower in Shakespeare's *Pericles* at Stratford-upon-Avon in 1958. In the event, it was performed by the West Indian Edric Conner, but the offer encouraged Robeson to play Othello at Stratford-upon-Avon the following season.

Errol John's *Moon on a Rainbow Shawl* won first prize in the 1957 *Observer* play competition, set up by its theatre critic Kenneth Tynan and judged by Tynan, Peter Hall, Alec Guinness, Peter Ustinov and Michael Barry, Head of BBC TV Drama. John came from Trinidad's cosmopolitan capital, Port-of-Spain, where he acted and wrote for the theatre. He arrived in London in 1951 to attend the Old Vic Theatre School and pursued his acting career in repertory and on radio, TV and film.

He wrote *Moon on a Rainbow Shawl* in 1955, revising it several times for submission to the *Observer*. He learnt of its success two days before returning to Trinidad – and cancelled his passage. Binkie Beaumont of H.M. Tennent, the West End's largest producer, had optioned the play, but saw it as uncommercial and passed it on to the Royal Court. Frith Banbury, the play's director, spent five weeks in the West Indies seeking a girl to play Rosa and absorbing the life of Port-of-Spain for Sainthill's crumbling set. John did a further rewrite to strengthen the dramatic development underlying his 'poetry', but he refused to change the title.

The action centres on two lovers, Ephraim and Rosa, and a married couple, Charlie and Sophia, and their struggles to escape the poverty and discrimination that oppress them. The ambitious Ephraim is keen to escape the slums and seek his fortune working on the buses in England, unencumbered by wife and family. Rosa, his pregnant girlfriend, wants him to settle down with her in Trinidad. Charlie, an outstanding cricketer, has damaged his career by opposing discrimination against black players. Now prey to drink, he steals money to buy a bicycle for his daughter, Esther, to enable her to take up her scholarship at a good school. Sophia, his scolding wife, gives vital moral support to him when the theft is discovered, as well as to Rosa on Ephraim's departure. Banbury's multiracial cast reflected Trinidad's cosmopolitan population and included stars such as Earle Hyman (Ephraim), John Bouie (Charlie) and Vinnette Carroll (Sophia), all of whom impressed *The Times*' reviewer.

But what of Errol John's play? Milton Shulman likened it to *Cry the Beloved Country* and *Porgy and Bess*, which try 'to hew out of drama the unquenchable spirit of the depressed and underprivileged Negro. What gives these plays their special quality is their irrepressible buoyancy in the face of overpowering adversity. They deal with characters who have to be hopeful because despair is their natural lot.' Irving Wardle detected this spirit in the 1988 Almeida revival directed by Maya Angelou. Comparing John's play with those of Irish writer Sean O'Casey, Wardle noted that 'where O'Casey closes up all escape routes, Mr John gives his characters a chance.' As one of the new Britons on the *Empire Windrush* observed in 1948: 'When the situation is desperate you take a chance – you don't wait until you die.'

In other areas, too, playwrights were exploring the legacy of British domination in their native countries. Born in Dublin in 1923, Brendan Behan had early experience of imprisonment for IRA activities, which gave him the material for his first play, *The Quare Fellow* (see chapter 10). The plot of his next play, *The Hostage*, revolved around the kidnapping of a young British soldier by the IRA. Behan called himself 'a Communist during the day and a Catholic at night'. His plays were influenced by Brecht but also contained much Irish humour. His last play, *Richard's Cork Leg*, was left unfinished at the time of his death in 1964.

86 *Flesh to a Tiger*
*Cleo Laine as Della and
Edgar Wreford as the
White Doctor, Royal
Court Theatre,
London, 1958
Photograph by
David Sim.*

First performed at the
Royal Court Theatre in
1958, *Flesh to a Tiger*
was notable for the
stage acting début of
jazz singer Cleo Laine
in the central role of
Della.

85 *Flesh to a Tiger*
*Set design by Loudon
Sainthill, Royal Court
Theatre, London, 1958
British Council
Collection
S.2412-1986*

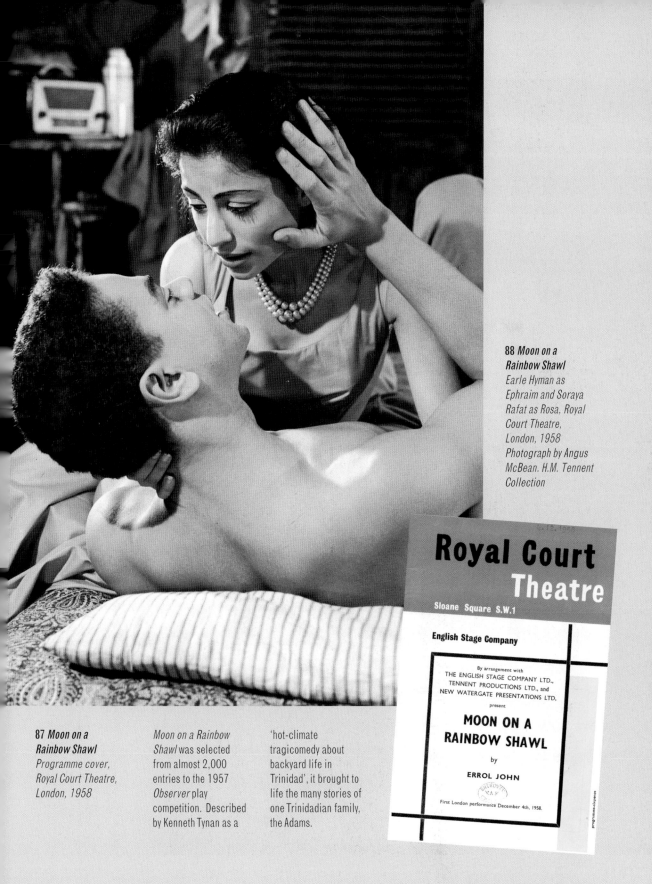

88 *Moon on a Rainbow Shawl*
Earle Hyman as Ephraim and Soraya Rafat as Rosa, Royal Court Theatre, London, 1958 Photograph by Angus McBean. H.M. Tennent Collection

Royal Court Theatre

Sloane Square S.W.1

English Stage Company

By arrangement with
THE ENGLISH STAGE COMPANY LTD.,
TENNENT PRODUCTIONS LTD., and
NEW WATERGATE PRESENTATIONS LTD.
present

MOON ON A RAINBOW SHAWL

by

ERROL JOHN

First London performance December 4th, 1958.

87 *Moon on a Rainbow Shawl*
Programme cover, Royal Court Theatre, London, 1958

Moon on a Rainbow Shawl was selected from almost 2,000 entries to the 1957 *Observer* play competition. Described by Kenneth Tynan as a 'hot-climate tragicomedy about backyard life in Trinidad', it brought to life the many stories of one Trinidadian family, the Adams.

89 Brendan Behan
1956
Photograph by
Denis Hughes-Gilbey

90 *The Hostage*
Murray Melvin (centre)
as the hostage Leslie,
Theatre Workshop,
Theatre Royal,
Stratford East, 1958
Photograph by
John Spinner

Joan Littlewood
introduced a new style
of production in which
the author's text might
be only a starting point
from which actors were
encouraged to
improvise and develop
their individuality. In a
loose structure such as
a Behan play, the
method often worked
well.

91 *The Hostage*
Set design by Sean Kenny, Wyndham's Theatre, London, 1959
British Council Collection
S.2268-1986

For *The Hostage*, Joan Littlewood found in Sean Kenny a designer who could realise her idea of a basic structure, through and round which her actors could 'flow'. Kenny's architectural training ensured a down-to-earth, bare-bones approach. His sparse three-dimensional set allowed the actor the freedom so essential to Littlewood's method of production.

Brendan Behan,
1956. Photograph by
Denis Hughes-Gilbey

'The same story was splashed across every front page: "BRITISH SOLDIER FOUND DEAD IN NICOSIA ... EIGHTEEN YEARS OLD ... A HOSTAGE". It was the first time we'd seen that word in a newspaper.
"It's like something from the past," said Beatrice [Behan].
"There's a play in it."
"I know nothing about Cyprus," said Brendan, "but I do know about Ireland."...
"Write it," I said.'

JOAN LITTLEWOOD, *JOAN'S BOOK* (1994)

'Satire is a sort of glass, wherein beholders do generally discover everybody's face but their own.'

JONATHAN SWIFT AS QUOTED BY HUMPHREY CARPENTER,
THAT WAS SATIRE THAT WAS (2000)

10 Man Bites God

As a member of the Irish Republican Army (IRA), Brendan Behan spent most of his youth in the 1940s in prison in England or Dublin. He used the time to learn Gaelic and the experience as the basis for his novel *Borstal Boy* and his play about capital punishment, *The Quare Fellow*. The play was first produced in London by Joan Littlewood in May 1956, within days of John Osborne's *Look Back in Anger* at the Royal Court. With his colourful past, Behan had to tread carefully between the British and Irish authorities, the press and the IRA, whose members stood for the Irish national anthem on the first night but sat through 'God Save the Queen', according to the *Daily Mail*. Playing down his talented family background, Behan presented himself as a nonconformist slum-boy-made-good who teased the Establishment and who gave the credit for *The Quare Fellow* to his fellow prisoners ('I did not write this play – the lags wrote it').

His play captivated the critics, creating a tension that Kenneth Tynan in the *Observer* found 'intolerable':

> But it is we who feel it, not the people in the play. We are moved precisely in the degree they are not. With superb dramatic tact, the tragedy is concealed beneath layer after layer of rough comedy … The curtain falls, but not before we have heard the swing and the jerk of the drop. I left the theatre feeling overwhelmed and thanking all the powers that be for Sydney Silverman.

Thanks to Silverman's campaign, capital punishment was eventually abolished, although not until December 1964.

In her recollection (quoted opposite) of Behan's next major play, *The Hostage* (see chapter 9), Joan Littlewood omitted to say that it was commissioned by Gael Linn, an organisation dedicated to the revival of Irish culture and Gaelic-speaking theatre. Despite the recent success of *The Quare Fellow* in London's West End, Behan showed commitment to the Irish cause by writing the play *An Giall* in Gaelic for production in Eire. Set in a Dublin brothel, it focuses on a kidnapped British

National Service soldier whom the IRA kill when one of their soldiers is hanged in Belfast. Translated into English as *The Hostage*, the play was staged at Stratford East by Joan Littlewood in October 1958.

In his *Sunday Times* review Harold Hobson noted:

> lines alleging the brutality of the British in Kenya, in India, in Cyprus that strike an Englishman across the face like a lash: and it has lines also about the fatal habit that the Irish have of blaming their incompetence on the English which will cause no joy in Eire. Mr Behan will anger the shortsighted in both countries; but to the discerning he gives a magnificent experience.

Taking 'the mickey out of English and Irish in equal proportions' (according to Richard Buckle) was a canny tactic that kept most critics on board. But where did Behan himself stand politically? His note in the programme guardedly suggests both a real compassion for people and deep anger at partition:

> [Behan] has hatred for the political forces who divide and subject Ireland: but for people – even if those people are the instruments of antagonistic political forces – he has only love and understanding.
>
> If a stranger attacks Britain, no one will support this country more strongly than Brendan Behan, but when he talks of Ireland – of a country where … partition gives such a sense of continuing betrayal and defeat that the brilliant and useful ones leave for abroad to escape the internecine quibbling and denigration – he grows angry with the anger of a man who loves his native place as passionately as Shakespeare loved his.

A revenge killing during the struggle for independence on Cyprus is said to have inspired *Serjeant Musgrave's Dance* (1959) by John Arden. Initially a failure at the Royal Court, the play is now regarded as an outstanding piece of modern drama. Set in Victorian Britain, it shows Musgrave and his men, deserters from a war in the colonies, returning the body of a dead comrade to the town of his birth. Their aim is to impress the obscenity of war upon the townspeople by killing twenty-five of them. Paradoxically, the pacifist cause involves shock – suspending a skeleton instead of a flag – and the threat of violence when a Gatling gun is pointed at the audience, triggering a fear that can only greet with relief the arrival of dragoons who restore order.

The 'puzzlement' of the play divided the critics. What seemed a 'frightful ordeal' to one was 'exciting, powerful and fascinating' to another. Ten days into the run, director Lindsay Anderson issued a leaflet asking 'What kind of a theatre do you want?' in which he quoted leading actors' and writers' enthusiastic support for the play. Arden later continued the debate in his introduction to the published text, concluding that

> complete pacifism is a very hard doctrine: and if this play appears to advo-
> cate it with perhaps some timidity, it is probably because I am naturally a
> timid man – and also because I know that if I am hit I very easily hit back:
> and I do not care to preach too confidently what I am not sure I can practise.

During the 1950s revue on the London stage was typified by shows such as *Jokers Wild* (1954) and *Clown Jewels* (1959) by the Crazy Gang. By 1959 the gang had been together for twenty-seven years and were all aged between sixty and seventy-two. They had long been threatening to retire but kept being persuaded to do one more show. Many agreed that the Gang's jokes were old and corny, and yet irresistibly funny because of the charm of the performers. A different but also highly popular type of 'intimate revue' was developed by John Cranko, a choreographer with the Sadler's Wells Ballet (see chapter 2).

As a form of theatrical and mass-media entertainment, satire took off between 1960 to 1963, with the setting up of the Establishment Club, London's first venue devoted to the genre, and the development of satirical television series such as *That Was The Week That Was*. Satire was the voice of youth, which since the Suez crisis in 1956 and the abolition of National Service in 1959 was becoming increasingly critical of the complacency of Harold Macmillan's Tory government.

In 1960 the revue *Beyond the Fringe* opened at the Edinburgh Festival. It featured Jonathan Miller and Peter Cook from Cambridge University and Alan Bennett and Dudley Moore from Oxford University. They wrote their own material, according to Alan Bennett, by all standing around and deciding what they loathed, then sending it up. Theirs was a new form of satirical revue performed without need for costume or make-up. They could be funny about anything they chose, opening up subjects previously thought risqué such as homosexuality, death, capital punishment or the Royal Family, and referring to living politicians by name. *Beyond the Fringe* revolutionised revue, taking London by storm when it transferred to the Fortune Theatre in 1961, then New York in 1962, before finally closing in the West End in 1966 after a record run of 2,200 performances.

92 *The Quare Fellow*
Maxwell Shaw as Dunlavin, Brian Murphy as the Man of Thirty, and Glynn Edwards as the Hard Case, Theatre Workshop, Theatre Royal, Stratford East, 1956
Photograph by Denis Hughes-Gilbey

A biographical note in the programme for Theatre Workshop's production of Brendan Behan's *The Quare Fellow* described Behan as 'A man of acute observation and perspicacity, [who] has known many men awaiting execution; in some cases he has talked with them until the day of their deaths.' The first-night audience included fifteen leaders of the pre-war Republican movement and two Special Branch detectives.

**93 Serjeant
Musgrave's Dance**
*Set design by Jocelyn
Herbert, Royal Court
Theatre, London, 1959
S.1055-1983*

The first production of
*Serjeant Musgrave's
Dance* was designed by
Jocelyn Herbert, who
worked extensively at
the Royal Court Theatre
and helped establish
the distinctive Royal
Court look. Herbert said
that 'There are so many
scenes in *Musgrave*

that it seemed to me
you had to do it with
very little so as not to
have over-long scene
changes and lose the
urgency of the text …
The first drawings were
more elaborate than the
last solution and at the
model stage we started
with a crane and a
barge for the first
scene on the canal
wharf and gradually got
down to nothing but a
ground row of weeds
and grass.'

**94 Serjeant
Musgrave's Dance**
*A page from the prompt
book used at the Royal
Court Theatre, London,
1959*

95 *Clown Jewels*
The Crazy Gang in their
spoof of the 'Ascot
scene' of My Fair Lady,
Victoria Palace
Theatre, London, 1959
Photograph by
Houston Rogers

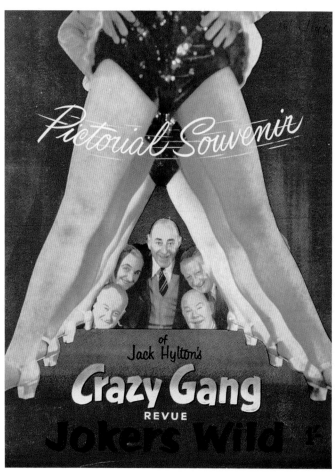

96 (left) *Jokers Wild*
Cover for the souvenir
programme, Victoria
Palace Theatre,
London, 1954
Photograph by
Houston Rogers

97 (above) *Jokers Wild*
Page from the souvenir
programme showing
the Crazy Gang as
Monks and 'Teddy
Boys', Victoria Palace
Theatre, London, 1954
Photograph by
Houston Rogers

98 *Beyond the Fringe*
Newspaper illustration
from The Sunday Times,
30 July 1961
Photographs by
Zoë Dominic

99 *Beyond the Fringe*
(left to right) Peter
Cook, Dudley Moore,
Alan Bennett and
Jonathan Miller,
Fortune Theatre,
London, 1961
Photograph by
Zoë Dominic

Beyond the Fringe
instigated a 1960s
satire boom and
launched international
theatre, television and
comedy careers for its
four stars.

Richard Harris
1957. Photograph
by John Spinner

'The shock of the new
agitated and appalled
these censors. The angry
young playwrights of the
1950s alarmed them. From
their reports and inter-
office memoranda of the
1960s it is not difficult to
glean the impression of a
group of like-minded men
standing firm against the
tide of what they
perceived to be "bearded
lefties" undermining all
that they held dear and
valuable in Britain. And
they fought to the very
end in this endeavour.'

NICHOLAS DE JONGH, *POLITICS, PRUDERY AND
PERVERSIONS: THE CENSORING OF THE ENGLISH STAGE
1901–1968 (2001)*

Not in Front of the Censor

Samuel Beckett's resistance to censorship resulted in major stand-offs between him and the Lord Chamberlain. The first of these in 1954 delayed the UK première of *Waiting for Godot* by over a year (see chapter 3). In 1958 months of wrangling over *Endgame*'s 'blasphemous' references to God as 'The Bastard – he doesn't exist' made headline news until Beckett gave in and replaced 'Bastard' with 'swine' (as suggested by the Lord Chamberlain). The *Evening Standard* fulminated: 'If Lord Scarborough wants to shed his powers of censorship over the theatre, he is going the right way about it … The only answer is to abolish the censorship and rely on the common law to deal with managements who abuse their freedom to put on obscene plays.'

Look Back in Anger, on the other hand, got past the Examiner quite swiftly in 1956. Indeed, its author believed that 'the Lord Chamberlain's Office must have misjudged certain elements as for years television critics and provincial newspapers were to complain about the earthy, degrading or even filthy language.' The only deletion he could remember was 'as tough as a night in a Bombay brothel and as rough as a matelot's arse'; in the event, 'arm' was substituted for 'arse'. One playgoer, who saw *Look Back in Anger* on tour in Torquay in 1957, wrote to the Home Secretary that it was 'a conception of a diseased and depraved mentality and the outpouring of a cesspool mind. I am at a loss to understand how this play could reach the English stage.' The complaint was forwarded to the Lord Chamberlain's Office, which, having licensed the play, acknowledged and filed the letter as evidence of audience reaction.

Policing nudity on stage also kept the Lord Chamberlain's Office busy, deterring those who tried to subvert the golden rule – 'if it moves it's rude' – with such warnings as 'Lord Clarendon will not permit breasts being visible when the girls are moving, either through flimsy covering, or on account of absence or of looseness of costume.' At the Windmill Theatre, Vivian van Damm's *Revudeville* shows sailed close to the wind before, during and after the Second World War without resulting in a prosecution. But the proliferation of new Soho strip clubs in the early 1960s led to diminishing audiences at the Windmill, whose shows were now considered staid in comparison, and the theatre closed in 1964. The former Comptroller to the Lord Chamberlain wrote to commiserate, adding mischievously: 'What will the London Morality Council do for their spare evenings? I shudder to think!'

Homosexuality, still illegal, became a subject of public debate and a major concern for the Lord Chamberlain in the mid-1950s, when the Wolfenden Committee was researching its *Report of the Committee on Homosexual Offences and Prostitution*. West End producers Donald Albery and Binkie Beaumont tested a loophole in the theatre club system, whereby private clubs could stage for members plays unlicensed by the Lord Chamberlain's Office. They turned the Comedy Theatre into a 'club' – the New Watergate – and presented unlicensed plays with homosexual content, including Arthur Miller's *A View from the Bridge* in October 1956, Tennessee Williams' *Cat on a Hot Tin Roof* and Robert Anderson's *Tea and Sympathy*.

In 1958 the Arts Theatre Club staged Roger Gellert's play *Quaint Honour*, which openly dealt with homosexuality in a British public school. Terence Rattigan considered his play *Ross*, based on the life story of T.E. Lawrence, as perhaps the most important of his career. His suggestion that it was Lawrence's guilt at his own homosexuality that led to his withdrawal from public life caused some problems with the Lord Chamberlain, but the play successfully opened at the Theatre Royal, Haymarket, in 1960. Even by 1964, Joe Orton's *Entertaining Mr Sloane*, often interpreted as a modern version of the Oedipus myth, was considered shocking when it first appeared at the New Arts Theatre Club. Liberal audiences of the 1960s still found it hard to take the play's combination of murder, mother love and homosexuality.

The New Watergate soon ran out of funds, but it had set a precedent that was used in the 1960s, notably when the Royal Court transformed itself into a 'club' to stage the uncensored version of Edward Bond's *Saved* in 1965, featuring the notorious stoning of a baby in a pram. Although the Lord Chamberlain brought a successful prosecution, director William Gaskill observed that the affair 'brought to a head the case against the Lord Chamberlain's power of pre-censorship. The following three years were dominated by the fight to break this power, a fight we eventually won.'

The publication of the Wolfenden Report in 1957 encouraged a climate in which the Lord Chamberlain partly relaxed the total ban on representing homosexuality on stage. The new policy was soon tested by Shelagh Delaney's inclusion of a young gay man in *A Taste of Honey* (1958) (see chapter 8). The relaxation, however, did not yet extend to lesbianism. The Lord Chamberlain continued to refuse a licence to Lillian Hellman's 1934 play *The Children's Hour* until 1960, six years before the major breakthrough came with *The Killing of Sister George* by Frank Marcus.

Portrayal of the Royal Family on stage was strictly banned. The Lord Chamberlain could also refuse to license a play that represented 'in an invidious manner a living person, or any person recently dead', or that was calculated 'to impair friendly relations with any Foreign Power'. John Johnston, a former Comptroller, observed that politicians became fair game by 1960 in revues such as *Beyond the Fringe* (see chapter 10), in which Peter Cook named and mimicked Prime Minister Harold Macmillan. He cited various examples of what constituted 'an invidious manner', including Rolf Hochhuth's *Soldiers*, which accused the late Winston Churchill of involvement in the death of his Polish ally General Sikorski. The surrounding controversy delayed any production of it in the UK until after the Lord Chamberlain's powers were abolished in 1968.

Another episode involving Churchill occurred in the 1957 Theatre Workshop production of *You Won't Always Be on Top*, a 'slice-of-life' play written by a builder, Henry Chapman, and set on a building site. The Lord Chamberlain prosecuted Chapman, Joan Littlewood, Gerry Raffles, Richard Harris and John Bury for performing a script that differed substantially from that approved by his office. No allowance was made for the fact that Joan Littlewood's rehearsal methods often involved major rewrites.

A defence fund was supported by the Earl of Harewood, George Devine, Peter Hall, Kenneth Tynan, Henry Sherek and others, and a QC was hired. The *Daily Telegraph*'s account of the proceedings at West Ham Magistrates' Court described 'a scene in which a character gave an impression of the opening of a public lavatory. The Lord Chamberlain's men took it that the actor was attempting to impersonate Sir Winston Churchill.' Or, in Joan Littlewood's version, Richard Harris 'peed into the open trapdoor while impersonating Winston Churchill'. All the accused pleaded guilty and were fined a total of less than £15. The Lord Chamberlain won, but it was Joan Littlewood who claimed it as 'Our victory … the real blow at the ancient institution of censorship'.

100 *Revudeville*
Cover of souvenir programme, Windmill Theatre, London, 1957

The Windmill was famous as the only theatre in London where full nudity was permitted. Not all the girls, however, were showgirls or nudes: between the nude scenes there were small ballets, sketches and stand-up comedians.

101 (lower left)
Quaint Honour
Cast list from the programme at the Arts Theatre Club, London, 1958

102 *Quaint Honour*
Newspaper photograph for the production performed at the Arts Theatre Club, London, 1958

QUAINT HONOUR

by
ROGER GELLERT

Robert Hallowes, a Housemaster ...... JOHN RICHMOND
M. L. Park, Head of House ...... PHILIP WADDILOVE
J. V. H. Tully, a House Prefect ...... JOHN CHARLESWORTH
R. R. Turner ⎱ Juniors ...... RODERICK McLAREN
T. A. B. Hamilton ⎰ ...... MICHAEL CARIDIA

The play directed by FRANK DUNLOP

Settings by PAUL MAYO

AUTHOR'S NOTE

If you try to write a realistic Public School play, you are fairly limited in subject matter. Most schoolboys—and not only the dim ones—are preoccupied with sport and sex. A few care more for poetry or grub, but these are interior pleasures and don't lend themselves to the stage. I thought it would be rewarding to consider the more basic issues.

These schoolboy relationships are unique and touching phenomena. It is well known—though some parents and teachers cultivate the Nelson touch—that the affairs are by no means always platonic. But I must add that there is no suggestion that any of the boys involved will be homosexual in adult life: rather the reverse. They are merely reacting in the natural and indeed the only possible way in highly unnatural circumstances. If we insist on segregating our children at their age of maximum sexual energy, we can hardly blame them for behaving as any healthy animal would.

The results, though, are more than animal: passions of infinite variety, strained by conflicting loyalties, and dyed deep with all the splendours and miseries of adolescence.

R. G.

The action of the play takes place in a Public School

ACT ONE
Scene 1   Hallows' Study on a Summer Evening.
Scene 2   Tully's Study, the next morning.
Scene 3   Tully's Study that afternoon.

ACT TWO
Scene 1   Tully's Study four days later; Sunday morning.
Scene 2   Hallows' Study the same morning.
Scene 3   Tully's Study. later.

Time : The present.

Posters designed and executed by Ian Emmerson. Scenery built and painted by Stage Decor Ltd. Furniture by the Old Times Furnishing Co. Ltd. Electrical equipment by Strand Electrical and Engineering Co. Ltd. Sound by StagesounD. Tinned food by Smedley's and Civil Service Stores. Guitar lent by Lew Davis. Properties by Robinsons. Nylon Stockings by Kayser. Wardrobe Care by Lux. Photographs of this production by Angus McBean. Virginia Cigarettes by Abdulla.

For the London Arts Theatre Committee Limited:
General Manager ... ... **Bernard Gillman**
Box Office Manager ... ... MARION PULLEM (TEM 3354)
Press Representative ... ... GEORGE PEARON (GER 1936)

Stage Director ... ... ROBERT HENRY
Stage Manager for "Quaint Honour" ... CLIVE WEBSTER
Assistant Stage Managers ... SONIA HIGGINS and BILL ALLAN
Master Carpenter ... ... EDWARD GOULD
Chief Electrician ... ... JOAN K. HARRIS

Three bells will be rung in the Foyer, Snack Bar & Lounge 3 minutes to curtain up.

Two bells will be rung in the Foyer, Snack Bar & Lounge 2 minutes to curtain up.

One bell will be rung in the Foyer, Snack Bar & Lounge 1 minute to curtain up.

NO SMOKING
You are requested not to smoke in the Auditorium
NOT EVEN ABDULLA VIRGINIA

1958

Tully (played by Mr. John Charlesworth, right) sees Hamilton (Mr. Michael Caridia) for a part in the school play. A scene from the Arts Theatre production of *Quaint Honour*.

103 *Ross*
Michael Bryant as T.E.
Lawrence and Richard
Warner as the Turkish
General, Theatre Royal,
Haymarket, 1961
Photograph by
Angus McBean

After some initial
problems with the Lord
Chamberlain, *Ross*
opened in 1960 with
Alec Guinness in the
title role. Michael
Bryant took over the
lead later in the run.

104 *Entertaining
Mr Sloane*
Dudley Sutton as
Sloane and Madge Ryan
as Kath, New Arts
Theatre Club, London,
1964
Photograph by
Anthony Crickmay

105 *The Children's Hour*
Patricia Healey as Mary, Jocelyn Britton as Peggy and Gillian Gale as Evelyn, Arts Theatre Club, London, 1956
Photograph by Houston Rogers

Although *The Children's Hour* was performed at the Arts Theatre in 1956 under club theatre conditions, it did not receive a major public performance in London until the production by the Royal National Theatre in 1994.

106 (lower right)
You Won't Always Be on Top
Richard Harris (centre) as Lofty, Theatre Workshop, Theatre Royal, Stratford East, 1957
Photograph by John Spinner

107 *You Won't Always Be on Top*
Theatre Workshop, Theatre Royal, Stratford East, 1957
Photograph by John Spinner

In her autobiography Joan Littlewood said of this play, 'There was no plot, no drama, just men going to work on a building site in the rain on a Monday morning, and the story of their day. We would have to cope with bricklaying, pipelaying, carpentry, scowing … the whole stage area from the back wall to the stalls, from side exit to loading bay, would have to be transformed. It was a challenge, to express the inexpressible with a few well-worn sayings picked up from a previous generation – but feelings as profound and strange as yours and mine.'

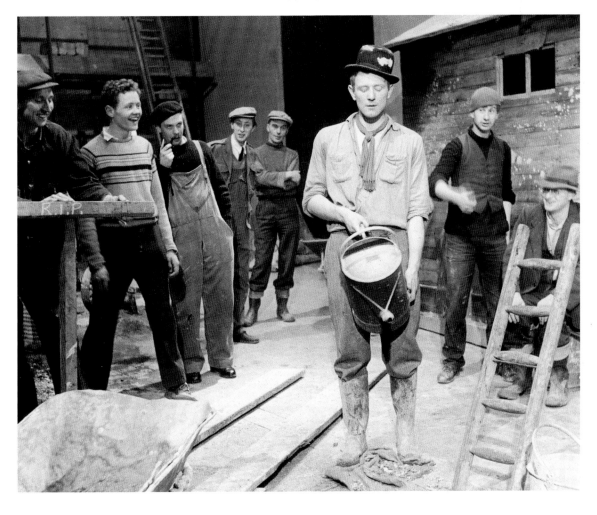

Robert Stephens as
Atahuallpa, Royal Hunt
of the Sun, 1964
Photograph by
Angus McBean

'What function does the theatre serve? What psychological nerve did it come out of? What is it there for? I think it's a kind of laboratory of the spirit and the soul, where as a group of people … you can share your sense of moral identity…. There is a connection between social dysfunction and the death of live theatre. There is a link between being purged and civilized by the collective experience.'

TIM PIGOTT-SMITH FROM KATE DUNN, *EXIT THROUGH THE FIREPLACE: THE GREAT DAYS OF REP* (1998)

12   1964 and All That

The urge for renewal in the post-war era stimulated not only new writing, but also the exploration of new performance spaces, alternatives to proscenium arch theatre, with performer and audience sharing one room. The growth in Arts Council grants from £820,000 in 1965 to £3,205,000 in 1968 reflected among other things increasing support for new playwrights, regional touring and the construction of new repertory theatres.

The Mermaid Theatre was originally set up in 1951 at the home of Bernard Miles in St John's Wood, London. The opening production was a performance of Purcell's opera *Dido and Aeneas*, starring the international soprano Kirsten Flagstad. During the 1953 Coronation festivities, Miles's Elizabethan-style stage was erected for performances in the Royal Exchange in the City of London. This proved so popular that the Corporation of London agreed in 1956 to lease him a disused warehouse in Puddle Dock. This was converted into a permanent theatre which opened successfully with the musical *Lock Up Your Daughters* in 1959. In Scarborough, the Library Theatre was founded in 1955 by Stephen Joseph, son of the actress Hermione Gingold and publisher Michael Joseph. While in America, Joseph had been impressed by several 'theatres-in-the-round' and was determined to introduce one to Britain. He was eventually able to establish a tiny theatre-in-the-round on the first floor of Scarborough Public Library, where it flourished.

The first new playhouse to be built after the war was the Belgrade, Coventry, in 1958, which heralded a building boom of some thirty civic theatres during the 1960s and 1970s. Community-based, with ample foyers, the Belgrade gave the world première of plays from Arnold Wesker's Trilogy before the Royal Court presented it as a whole. In 1965 the Belgrade became the first UK theatre to pioneer theatre-in-education.

Laurence Olivier opened Britain's first major thrust-stage theatre at Chichester in 1962, prior to setting up the National Theatre at the Old Vic the following year. Also in 1962 Stephen Joseph's theatre-in-the-round found permanent form in an ex-cinema, the Victoria in Stoke-on-Trent. The year 1963 saw the Fringe movement stirring in Edinburgh with Jim Haynes's Traverse

Theatre, followed in 1964 by the Liverpool Everyman, which brought 'alternative' repertory theatre to young people and spawned studio theatres across the UK. The mix of contemporary and traditional spaces was later reflected in the National Theatre's three auditoria – the Cottesloe (studio), Olivier (open stage) and Lyttelton (proscenium) – when it opened on the South Bank in 1976–7.

Today, when performance is almost as likely to take place in a tramshed or quarry as in a theatre, it is an interesting coincidence that those powerhouses of modern British drama, the Theatre Workshop and the English Stage Company, both operated from proscenium arch theatres dating from the 1880s. For both those companies 1964–5 was a watershed. In autumn 1964, following a year-long West End run of *Oh! What a Lovely War*, the Theatre Royal, Stratford East, was leased to other managements for three years. Although another success was to follow in 1967 with *Mrs Wilson's Diary*, Joan Littlewood's involvement with Theatre Workshop lessened and ended in 1973-4. George Devine had succeeded in opening the Royal Court Theatre Studio, but the Royal Court was ceding key directors (Bill Gaskill, John Dexter) and actors (Joan Plowright, Colin Blakely, Robert Stephens, Frank Finlay) to the National Theatre, which even tried to recruit Devine himself. Although John Osborne came to the rescue with *Inadmissible Evidence* in 1964, followed by *A Patriot for Me*, a sudden heart attack ended Devine's reign in July 1965, and Bill Gaskill took over.

Peter Hall had from the early 1960s brought in Royal Court directors such as Bill Gaskill and designers like Jocelyn Herbert to work at the Royal Shakespeare Company, as well as Theatre Workshop designer John Bury, and relations between the four subsidised companies were close. The National Theatre, for instance, had a huge hit in 1964 with its first contemporary play, Peter Shaffer's *The Royal Hunt of the Sun*. Directed by John Dexter, its searching script, spectacular design by Michael Annals and Robert Stephens's unforgettable Atahuallpa effectively 'scaled the Andes' in taking epic theatre to new heights.

The RSC was riding high on several fronts. The Hall/Bury partnership created the groundbreaking production of Shakespeare's seven history plays, *The Wars of the Roses*, that rivalled Olivier's Othello at the National in the 400th anniversary celebrations of Shakespeare's birth in April 1964. It also hosted in 1964 the first of Peter Daubeny's World Theatre Seasons, a showcase of international performance by visiting foreign companies that was held annually at the Aldwych until 1975. Peter Hall, when Director of the National Theatre, appointed Thelma Holt to bring leading foreign companies to the South Bank. Since 1981 Lucy Neal and Rose Fenton have also emulated the indefatigable Peter

Daubeny with their biennial London International Festival of Theatre (LIFT).

Hall's 1960s RSC policy of staging Shakespeare at Stratford-upon-Avon while fostering modern drama and classics in London at the Aldwych had, together with the National Theatre's repertoire, added a new dimension to theatregoing in the West End. A glance at the Aldwych offering in *Theatre World*'s 'Quick Theatre Guide' for October 1964 reveals some extraordinary productions: David Rudkin's *Afore Night Come*, Harold Pinter's *The Birthday Party*, Samuel Beckett's *Endgame*, Christopher Marlowe's *The Jew of Malta*, Henry Livings's *Eh?*, Roger Vitrac's *Victor* and Peter Weiss's *Marat/Sade*. In addition, Joe Orton's début play, *Entertaining Mr Sloane*, had recently made it into the West End, thanks to a £3,000 investment by Terence Rattigan.

To win global renown for Peter Brook's production of the *Marat/Sade*, the experimental 'Theatre of Cruelty' season and Peter Hall's *The Wars of the Roses* was a great birthday present for Shakespeare, the RSC and British theatre. In just ten years it had found a new drama, major new playwrights, choreographers and satirists, and had evolved its own popular music that climaxed in The Beatles' invasion of America. It had developed state subsidy that acknowledged 'the right to fail', created the long-awaited National Theatre, built new regional theatres and made rep viable once more. It had also discovered new actors, playwrights, directors and designers, and given a voice to young men, women, black and working-class people, people from the regions and the Commonwealth.

British theatre in the decade 1955–64 had successfully undermined stage censorship and encouraged public debate about such issues as homosexuality, capital punishment, pacifism and even the very nature of language itself. Britain, which had once ruled the waves almost without thinking, was breaking out, feeling creative again, *making* waves – instead of just receiving American waves, French waves, German waves. While losing an empire, Britain was discovering herself, listening to her young people, their passions and their song. The nation was getting real, and theatre was both leading and mirroring the process.

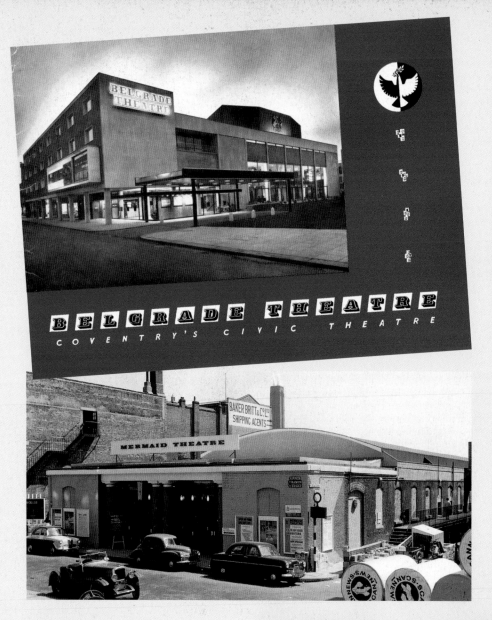

108 (top left) Brochure cover for the opening of the Belgrade Theatre, Coventry
1958

The Belgrade Theatre, Coventry, was part of a large-scale local redevelopment after the city had been partially destroyed by enemy bombing. The theatre acquired its name in recognition of a gift of timber from the Yugoslav city of Belgrade that was used in the construction of the auditorium.

109 (left) The Mermaid Theatre, London
1959

110 (right) Postcard showing the interior of Chichester Festival Theatre
1962

Surrounded by parkland, Chichester Festival Theatre was the first modern theatre in Britain to incorporate an Elizabethan-style open 'thrust' stage, allowing the audience a close involvement with the performers. The first season, directed by Sir Laurence Olivier, included a celebrated production of Chekhov's *Uncle Vanya*.

111 **The Royal Hunt of the Sun**
Robert Stephens as Atahuallpa and Colin Blakely as Pizarro, Chichester Festival Theatre, 1964 Photograph by Angus McBean

1955-1964 Timeline

Note: 'First performance' indicates the first performance in the UK unless stated otherwise.

1955

January 10th – Marian Anderson becomes the first black singer to perform at the Metropolitan Opera, New York

January 18th – Premiere of Kenneth MacMillan's ballet *Danses Concertantes*

January 27th – First performance of Michael Tippett's *A Midsummer Marriage*

April 5th – Winston Churchill resigns as Prime Minister

April 18th – Albert Einstein dies

April – Industrial action hits Fleet Street

May 14th – Formation of the Warsaw Pact

May 26th – The Conservatives win the general election

May 31st – The Government declares a state of emergency following the dock and rail strikes

June 16th – First performance of Orson Welles' *Moby Dick*

June 30th – First performance of Bertolt Brecht's *Mother Courage*

July 13th – Ruth Ellis is the last woman to be hanged in the UK

July 18th – Disneyland opens in California

August 3rd – First performance of Samuel Beckett's *Waiting for Godot*

September 6th – The Cyprus emergency

September 19th – Military coup in Argentina overthrows Peron

September 22nd – Independent TV begins

September 30th – James Dean dies in car crash

October 31st – Princess Margaret decides not to marry Peter Townsend

December 19th – First performance of John Cranko's *Cranks*

1956

February 9th – First performance of Brecht and Weill's *The Threepenny Opera*

February 29th – Rosa Parks is arrested in Alabama for refusing to sit in the 'blacks only' area of a bus

March 6th – Electrification of the railways in the UK is announced.

April 9th – First performance of Arthur Miller's *The Crucible*

April 11th – First performance of Enid Bagnold's *The Chalk Garden*

April 19th – Wedding of Grace Kelly and Prince Rainier III in Monaco

May 5th – Sadler's Wells Ballet celebrates its 25th anniversary

May 8th – First performance of John Osborne's *Look Back in Anger*

May 8th – First performance of Roland Petit's *La Chambre*

May 24th – First performance of Brendan Behan's *The Quare Fellow*

June 3rd – Third class rail carriages are abolished

July 5th – The Clean Air Act is passed

August – The Suez Crisis

August 14th – Bertolt Brecht dies

August 29th – The Berliner Ensemble season opens in London

September 3rd – Ram Gopal performs at the Edinburgh Festival

September 11th – Teddy Boy riots

October 3rd – The Bolshoi Ballet season opens at Covent Garden with *Romeo and Juliet*

October 11th – First performance of Arthur Miller's *A View from the Bridge*

October 26th – The Hungarian uprising

October 29th – Israel invades Sinai

November 5th – Soviet Russia crushes the Hungarian uprising

1957

January 1st – First performance of John Cranko's *The Prince of the Pagodas*

January 9th – Harold Macmillan becomes Prime Minister

January 16th – The Royal Ballet, created by charter from the Sadler's Wells Ballet, comes into being

April 10th – First performance of John Osborne's *The Entertainer*

April 22nd – First performance of

Jean Genet's *The Balcony*

May 14th – Emergency petrol rationing ends

May 31st – Arthur Miller is convicted of contempt of Congress after refusing to name names to House of Un-American Activities Committee.

June 1st – First Premium bond draw

July 6th – Althea Gibson becomes the first black Wimbledon tennis champion

September 4th – The Wolfenden Report of the Committee on Homosexual Offences and Prostitution is published

October 9th – First performance of Henry Chapman's *You Won't Always Be on Top*

October 17th – Windscale nuclear leak

October 24th – Death of Christian Dior

November 3rd – Laika the dog is launched into space by the Soviet Union

December 20th – Elvis is drafted into the USA Army

December 25th – First TV transmission of Queen's Christmas speech

1958

January 2nd – First performance of Kenneth MacMillan's *The Burrow*

January 30th – First performance of Tennessee Williams' *Cat on a Hot Tin Roof*

February 9th – The Lord Chamberlain refuses a licence for Samuel Beckett's *Endgame*

March 18th – The last débutantes are presented at court

March 27th – The Belgrade Theatre, Coventry opens

April 7th – CND Aldermaston march

April 22nd – Opening of the British West Indies Federation parliament

April 22nd – First performance of Mankovitz and More's *Expresso Bongo*

April 29th – First performance of Lerner and Loewe's *My Fair Lady*

May 1st – First performance of Roger Gellert's *Quaint Honour*

May 9th – Luchino Visconti's

production of Verdi's *Don Carlos* opens at Covent Garden

May 19th – First London performance of Harold Pinter's *The Birthday Party*

May 21st – First performance of Barry Reckord's *Flesh to a Tiger*

May 27th – First performance of Shelagh Delaney's *A Taste of Honey*

June 9th – Gatwick Airport opens

July 16th – First performance of Peter Shaffer's *Five Finger Exercise*

September 8th – Notting Hill race riots

September 16th – First performance of Tennessee Williams' *Suddenly Last Summer*

September 24th – First performance of Eugene O'Neill's *Long Day's Journey into Night*

September 30th – First performance of John Arden's *Live like Pigs*

October 14th – First performance of Brendan Behan's *The Hostage*

October 21st – The first Lady Peers are introduced in the House of Lords

October 27th – First performance of Frederick Ashton's *Ondine*

October 28th – Pope John XXIII elected

October 28th – First performance of Samuel Beckett's *Krapp's Last Tape* and *Endgame*

November 6th – The Lord Chamberlain ends the ban on plays with a homosexual subject

December 4th – First performance of Errol John's *Moon on a Rainbow Shawl*

December 12th – First performance of Leonard Bernstein's *West Side Story*

December 21st – De Gaulle becomes Prime Minister in France

1959

January 2nd – Fidel Castro proclaims a new government for Cuba

February 3rd – Buddy Holly, JP 'Big Bopper' Richardson and Richie Valens die in a plane crash

February 15th – First performance of Frank Norman and Lionel Bart's

Fings Ain't Wot They Used T'Be

March 30th – The Dalai Lama flees to India after China invades Tibet

April 7th – Paul Robeson performs Othello at Stratford

April 21st – Dame Margot Fonteyn arrested under suspicion of complicity in a planned coup in Panama

May 5th – First performance of John Osborne's *The World of Paul Slickey*

May 14th – First performance of Tennessee Williams' *Orpheus Descending*

May 25th – First performance of Arnold Wesker's *Roots*

May 28th – The Mermaid Theatre, London opens

July 17th – Death of Billie Holiday

August 4th – First performance of Lorraine Hansberry's *A Raisin in the Sun*

August 18th – The Mini motorcar introduced

September 6th – First performance of Arnold Wesker's *The Kitchen*

October 9th – The Conservatives win the General Election

October 22nd – First performance of John Arden's *Serjeant Musgrave's Dance*

November 2nd – Opening of the M1 Motorway

1960

January 21st – First performances of Harold Pinter's *The Room* and *The Dumb Waiter*

January 28th – First performance of Frederick Ashton's *La Fille mal Gardée*

March 21st – Sharpeville massacre in South Africa

April 27th – First performance of Harold Pinter's *The Caretaker*

April 28th – First performance of Eugène Ionesco's *Rhinoceros*

May 5th – Russia admits to shooting down an American U2 plane

May 6th – Wedding of Princess Margaret to Antony Armstrong-Jones

May 15th – First performance of Terence Rattigan's *Ross*

June 11th – First performance of Benjamin Britten's *A Midsummer Night's Dream*

June 30th – First performance of Lionel Bart's *Oliver!*

July 1st – First performance of Robert

Bolt's *A Man for All Seasons*

August 22nd – *Beyond the Fringe* performed at the Edinburgh Festival

November 2nd – *Lady Chatterley's Lover* published after the lifting of an obscenity ban

November 9th – John F. Kennedy elected as President of the USA

November 10th – First performance of Kenneth MacMillan's *The Invitation*

December 9th – First television broadcast of *Coronation Street* on Granada TV

1961

January 30th – The contraceptive pill goes on sale in the UK

March 20th – The Shakespeare Memorial Theatre at Stratford-upon-Avon becomes the Royal Shakespeare Theatre

April 11th – The Adolf Eichman trial commences in Israel

April 12th - Yuri Gagarin becomes the first man in space

May 10th – *Beyond the Fringe* opens in London

June 16th – Rudolf Nureyev defects in Paris following the Kirov Ballet's first performances in the West.

July 11th – First performance of Jean Anouilh's *Becket*

July 27th – First performance of John Osborne's *Luther*

August 20th – The Berlin Wall is built

September 14th – The first Mothercare shop opens in Kingston

October 9th – First performance of Anne Jellicoe's *The Knack*

October 24th – First performance of Edward Albee's *The American Dream*

November 2nd – Rudolf Nureyev makes his London début

November 25th – *The Mousetrap* celebrates the 10th anniversary of its first performance

1962

January 14th – Outbreak of smallpox in the UK

February 4th – The first *Sunday Times* colour supplement is published

April 27th – First performance of Arnold Wesker's *Chips with Everything*

May 3rd – First performance of Kenneth MacMillan's *The Rite of Spring*

May 8th – The last trolley buses are taken out of service

May 25th – The new Coventry Cathedral is consecrated

June 2nd – Britain's first legal casino, The Metropole, opens in Brighton

July 3rd – Algeria becomes independent from France

July 3rd – The Chichester Festival Theatre opens

August 5th – Death of Marilyn Monroe

August 6th – Jamaica becomes independent from the UK

August 9th – Sir Laurence Olivier becomes the first director of the National Theatre

August 31st – Trinidad and Tobago become independent from the UK

October 15th – Amnesty International is founded in London

October 22nd – The Cuban missile crisis

November 24th – First BBC TV broadcast of *That Was The Week That Was*

1963

January 12th – The Beatles' single *Please Please Me* is released

February 11th – Death of Sylvia Plath

March 12th – First performance of Frederick Ashton's *Marguerite and Armand*

March 19th – First performance of Joan Littlewood's *Oh! What a Lovely War*

March 27th – The Beeching Report implements large-scale cuts in UK rail service

June 3rd – Death of Pope John XXIII

June 5th – John Profumo, Secretary of State for War, resigns from Government after admitting to lying to Parliament

June 16th – Valentine Tereshkova becomes the first woman in space

June 21st – Pope Paul VI elected in Rome

August 8th – The Great Train Robbery

August 9th – First television broadcast on *Ready, Steady – Go!*

August 26th – Martha Graham and Company perform at the Edinburgh Festival

August 28th – Martin Luther King leads a 200,000 civil rights march on Washington

October 10th – Harold Macmillan resigns as Prime Minister

October 22nd – The National Theatre opens at the Old Vic with a performance of *Hamlet*

November 1st – First television broadcast of *Dr Who* on the BBC

November 22nd – President Kennedy is assassinated in Dallas

December 18th – First performance of Peter Darrell's *Mods and Rockers*

1964

January 12th – The Royal Shakespeare Company *Theatre of Cruelty* Season opens

January 21st – Maria Callas performs in *Tosca* at Covent Garden

February 6th – First performance of Edward Albee's *Who's Afraid of Virginia Woolf?*

February 8th – The Beatles arrive in the USA

March 20th – Death of Brendan Behan

March 28th – Radio Caroline begins transmissions from a ship in the North Sea

April 21st – BBC2 is launched

May 6th – First performance of Joe Orton's *Entertaining Mr Sloane*

May 18th – Mods and Rockers clash in Margate

June 14th – Nelson Mandela is sentenced to life imprisonment in South Africa for treason

July 6th – The Beatles' film *A Hard Day's Night* is premièred in London

July 7th – First performance of Peter Shaffer's *The Royal Hunt of the Sun*

August 20th – First performance of Peter Weiss's *Marat/Sade*

September 9th – First performance of John Osborne's *Inadmissible Evidence*

September 28th – The *Sun* newspaper published for the first time

October 16th – The Labour Party wins the general election and Harold Wilson becomes Prime Minister

October 24th – Martin Luther King is awarded the Nobel Peace Prize

October 31st – The Windmill Theatre closes

November 9th – Judy Garland and Liza Minelli appear together at the London Palladium

December 21st – MPs vote to abolish the death sentence in the UK

December 22nd – Cliff Richard, The Shadows and Una Stubbs appear in *Aladdin* at the London Palladium

Further Reading

Deirdre Bair, *Samuel Beckett: A Biography* (1978)

Christopher Booker, *The Neophiliacs* (1969)

Peter Brook, *Threads of Time: A Memoir* (1999)

Humphrey Carpenter, *That Was Satire That Was* (2000)

Charles Duff, *The Lost Summer: The Heyday of the West End Theatre* (1995)

John Elsom, *Post-war British Theatre* (revised 1979)

Richard Findlater (ed.), *At the Royal Court: 25 Years of the English Stage Company* (1981)

Juliet Gardiner, *From the Bomb to the Beatles: The Changing Face of Post-war Britain 1845–1965* (1999)

Howard Goorney, *The Theatre Workshop Story* (1981)

Peter Hall, *Making an Exhibition of Myself* (1993)

Bill Harry, *The British Invasion: How The Beatles and other UK Bands Conquered America* (2004)

Robert Hewison, *In Anger: Culture in the Cold War 1945–60* (1981)

Christopher Innes, *Modern British Drama 1890–1990* (1992)

John Johnston, *The Lord Chamberlain's Blue Pencil* (1990)

Nicholas de Jongh, *Politics, Prudery and Perversion: The Censoring of the English Stage 1901–1968* (2000)

Michael Kustow, *Peter Brook: A Biography* (2005)

Oscar Lewenstein, *Kicking Against the Pricks* (1994)

Peter Lewis, *The 50s* (1978)

Joan Littlewood, *Joan's Book: Joan Littlewood's Peculiar History As She Tells It* (1994)

Charles Marowitz et.al., *The Encore Reader: A Chronicle of the New Drama* (1965; repr. 1970)

Ulick O'Connor, *Brendan Behan* (1970)

John Osborne, *Almost a Gentleman* (1991)

Dan Rebellato, *1956 And All That: The Making of Modern British Drama* (1999)

Tony Richardson, *Long Distance Runner* (1993)

Dominic Shellard, *Kenneth Tynan: A Life* (2003)

John Russell Taylor, *Anger and After* (1962; 1963)

Wendy and J.C. Trewin, *The Arts Theatre, London 1927–1981* (1986)

Kenneth Tynan, *Tynan on Theatre* (1961; 1964)

Irving Wardle, *The Theatres of George Devine* (1978)

Arnold Wesker, *As Much As I Dare: An Autobiography 1932–1959* (1994)

Picture Credits

Index